The Se
Happiness

Tanushree Podder

Prolific author of books on
Mind, Body & Spirit

PUSTAK MAHAL®
Delhi • Bangalore • Mumbai • Patna • Hyderabad

Publishers
Pustak Mahal®, Delhi-110006

Sales Centres
- 6686, Khari Baoli, Delhi-110006, *Ph:* 23944314, 23911979
- 10-B, Netaji Subhash Marg, Daryaganj, New Delhi-110002
  Ph: 23268292, 23268293, 23279900 • *Fax:* 011-23280567
  E-mail: rapidexdelhi@indiatimes.com

Administrative Office
J-3/16 (Opp. Happy School), Daryaganj, New Delhi-110002
Ph: 23276539, 23272783, 23272784 • *Fax:* 011-23260518
E-mail: info@pustakmahal.com • *Website:* www.pustakmahal.com

Branch Offices
BANGALORE: 22/2, Mission Road (Shama Rao's Compound),
Bangalore-560027, *Ph:* 22234025 • *Fax:* 080-22240209
E-mail: pmblr@sancharnet.in • pustak@sancharnet.in

MUMBAI: 23-25, Zaoba Wadi (Opp. VIP Showroom), Thakurdwar,
Mumbai-400002, *Ph:* 22010941 • *Fax:* 022-22053387
E-mail: rapidex@bom5.vsnl.net.in

PATNA: Khemka House, 1st Floor (Opp. Women's Hospital), Ashok
Rajpath, Patna-800004 , *Ph:* 3094193 • *Telefax:* 0612-2302719
E-mail: rapidexptn@rediffmail.com

HYDERABAD: 5-1-707/1, Brij Bhawan, Bank Street, Koti,
Hyderabad-500095, *Ph:* 24737530 • *Fax:* 040-24737290
E-mail: pustakmahalhyd@yahoo.co.in

© Author

ISBN 81-223-0856-2

Edition : October 2004

Printed at : Param Offsetters, Okhla, New Delhi-110020

Dedication

This book is dedicated to my spouse
who has been a true mate and friend.
He is instrumental in bringing sunshine
and happiness into my life.
He has given me hope whenever
I have lost it; he has shaken me
out of cynicism whenever
I have fallen prey to it.

Contents

Introduction 9

1. What is Happiness? 13
2. One Simple Truth: Anyone Can Be Happy 15
3. Avoid Boredom 19
4. Accept Yourself 20
5. Be Optimistic 22
6. Turning Disadvantages into Success 24
7. Dealing with Failures 26
8. Focus on Your Strengths 28
9. Find an Inspiration 29
10. Mental Regimen 31
11. Momentous Moments 33
12. Treat People Right 35
13. Give Till You Ache 37
14. This is Life 39
15. Why Me? 40
16. A Matter of Attitude 41
17. How to Remain Positive 43
18. Attitudinal Tuning 45
19. Switch on the Smile 47
20. Get a Grip Over Your Mood 49
21. Control Your Emotions… 50
22. …But Don't Repress Them 52
23. Seek Good, Ignore Shortcomings 53
24. Accept What You Can't Change 55
25. There Are No Shortcuts 57

26. I Want More, Right Now! 58
27. Forgive and Forget 60
28. Be Humble and Generous 63
29. Stop Nitpicking 65
30. Nothing is Permanent 66
31. Learn to Laugh at Problems 67
32. Every Problem has a Solution 69
33. Time is the Greatest Healer 71
34. Discover God in Every Soul 73
35. Ethics and Morality 75
36. Carpé Diem 76
37. Keep Life Simple 77
38. Time for Introspection 78
39. Know Your Strengths 80
40. Keep Expectations Low 82
41. Don't Short Sell Yourself 84
42. Don't Seek Perfection 86
43. Sleep Like a Baby 88
44. Know Your Priorities 90
45. Manage Time Efficiently 92
46. Energy Highs and Lows 94
47. Strength and Courage 96
48. Loneliness Can be Depressing 98
49. Investing in Others 100
50. Giving Brings Joy 101
51. Nurture Your Marriage 103
52. Be More Social 104
53. Children Ensure Happiness 106
54. Care for Your Parents 107
55. Develop Creative Hobbies 108

56. Religion and Prayer 109
57. Lead a Stress-free Life 111
58. Happiness is Within You 113
59. Develop Strong Self-esteem 114
60. Don't Dwell in the Past; Live in the Present 116
61. Learn to Say 'No' 117
62. Be Flexible 119
63. Live for Today, Love for Tomorrow 121
64. Always Remember Someone with More Problems 123
65. Fight Anxiety 124
66. Control Anger 126
67. Control Greed 128
68. Don't Brood 129
69. Be Patient 131
70. Help Someone 133
71. Accept Criticism 135
72. Cherish Sincere Praise 136
73. Do Your Best and Forget the Rest 137
74. Work on Your Communication 138
75. Adapt to Change 140
76. Coping with Crisis 142
77. Listen to Your Heart 143
78. Relax and Recoup 144
79. Catch Up with Old Friends 145
80. Be Open to Learning 146
81. Be Your Natural Self 148
82. Release Pent-up Emotions 150
83. Unhappiness Causes Most Ailments 152
84. What is the Worst that Can Happen? 154
85. Busy People Don't Worry 155

86.	Put Your Problems in Writing	157
87.	Face the Inevitable	159
88.	Conquer Fears and Phobias	161
89.	Stop Criticising	163
90.	Everything is Minor	165
91.	Develop a Sense of Contentment	167
92.	Live with Your Conscience	168
93.	Seek Stability	170
94.	Earn Goodwill and Blessings	172
95.	Read Something Inspiring Each Day	173
96.	Forego Revenge	175
97.	Live with Nature	176
98.	Zip Your Lip	178
99.	Count Your Blessings	179
100.	Beat Depression and Become Cheerful	180
101.	20 Tips for Happiness	183
	Inspirational Quotes	185
	Epilogue	187

Introduction

"Ah! Happiness!" exclaimed my friend. "So, you are writing a book about happiness? Tell me – is anyone happy in this world? I think there is no happiness in this world. We all live in constant search of that elusive element," he ended cynically.

"Are you unhappy?" I asked, curious about his statement.

"Not really! But I'm not happy, either," he replied, after thinking for a moment.

He was right. So many of us are neither happy nor unhappy; we are living in an undecipherable condition. Most of the time, we do not know what we want. Happiness is an intangible state of mind that is difficult to define. It is an elusive state of Utopia that we crave for constantly, all through our lives.

Again, happiness means different things to different people. To some, it may just mean the ability to ensure three square meals a day. If they are able to get those meals, they are happy. To others, it may be experienced when they acquire a new car or a new house. To a few, it may mean establishing a perfectly compatible relationship with their spouse or family members. To each of us, the word 'happiness' has different connotations.

However, a state of happiness does not last forever. If I am happy today, it doesn't mean I will be happy tomorrow. It also doesn't mean that happiness doesn't have an everlasting quality! It is just that our concept of happiness keeps changing every few days. If a certain thing brings joy and happiness into our lives today, we may find something else missing tomorrow and may become unhappy yet again. This leads to an unending quest for the illusive quality called happiness, with the parameters and definition changing constantly.

Therefore, man is in constant search for happiness. He will devour books written on the subject, seek blessings from godmen, and attend any lecture or seminar that promises to reveal the path to joy and happiness.

But what *is* happiness? In my opinion, *happiness is just a state of mind*. You are only as happy as your mind allows you to be. If you are in a state of restlessness, how can you be happy?

There are no magic wells to provide water that can ensure happiness, nor are there any mantras that will impart joy when recited continuously. It is only by developing a positive attitude towards life that one can be happy. To develop the state of mental peace and contentment, people need to look inwards and not outwards. They need to find peace within themselves because peace and contentment are not available in the market, no matter what price one is willing to pay. Happiness is not a prescription drug. One doesn't have to work hard to acquire it nor go seeking it in the Himalayas. Either it is within you and you learn to discover it, or it will never be yours.

Recall the story of the musk deer searching tirelessly for the musk that smells so good; little does it realise that the aromatic musk lies within itself! A human being also spends his lifetime looking for things that will ensure him happiness and joy without realising that happiness lies within himself, waiting to be discovered.

If finding happiness were so easy, why would so many people remain unhappy? The truth is that it is not so easy to find this elusive gem. You can achieve wealth, position, status, social recognition, almost anything, but achieving satisfaction, joy and happiness seem ever so difficult. Why? I think it is simply because we are so intent on achieving materialistic things that we just don't have enough time to discover the joy of living – the happiness of being blessed by God. We never think of the blessings we have received from Him in terms of health and life. It is only when we see a handicapped person that we realise we are fortunate in having our limbs intact. But do we thank God for making us normal and healthy? We don't. Because we take it for granted. Similarly, there are many other things that we take for granted in life.

As long as we remain unaware of the things we have been blessed with, we can't be happy. We crave more and more materialistic things but ignore the greater value of the intangibles.

Many of my friends and family members asked me why I decided to write a book on such a difficult topic. I admit, it is difficult to write a book on happiness, simply because there are no guidelines, no research, no facts and figures that one can rely on. It is simply a matter of relating to the subject in your own way, relying on the heart and its dictates. But I had a reason for writing on this subject and I'll share it with readers. I am writing because I had suffered many incidents of frustration, unhappiness and disquiet for years – until I found a way to deal with them. I won't say I discovered the secrets of happiness or found the way to eternal peace but I have come a little closer to discovering it.

I have seen friends grieving over the loss of a close one; seen people get overwhelmingly depressed because they have lost a job or suffered some ailment. These can be extremely disturbing for people who can't handle such problems and end up needing the help of counsellors. Many of them become emotional wrecks and resort to various medications like tranquillisers and sleep-inducing drugs. It is not easy to deal with the downside of life. In fact, it is easier to advise than to practise.

I have experienced life's blows at close quarters. I have seen my loved ones die; I have seen my life go through mayhem and turmoil of the worst kind. There were times when I didn't want to live any more. But better sense prevailed and I began hunting for ways and means to deal with ups and downs in life. I went through the gamut of going to spiritual assemblies, seeking out truth, attending classes on various forms of spiritual practices like Vipassana, yoga, meditation, Reiki, Pranic healing etc. I ran from pillar to post seeking a practice that would bring peace and serenity to my heart. It took immense patience and fortitude, and there were many occasions when I almost gave up. It is so easy to throw in the towel and so difficult to strive and struggle.

In the end, I overcame the reverses and turned my life around towards the light of progress and happiness. I can't claim that adversities do not disturb me, or that I don't cry over them. But I get over them and that wins half the battle.

No one can discover happiness simply by reading books. It needs a more determined effort than the mere reading of words. It requires the implementation of suggestions; it entails an acceptance of things around us. The purpose of writing this book stretches beyond the visible endeavour of delineating codes of happiness. It encompasses the need to bring a little light into otherwise gloomy lives. In my quest for solace and joy, I discovered some simple truths. It is these truths that I am keen on sharing with readers.

I am neither a seer nor a preacher but a normal human being with my own share of woes which I am constantly struggling to overcome; but in the process of having spent half a century in this world I have discovered a few tenets which lead to the path of happiness and it is these tenets that I want to share with readers. If I am able to infuse even a single heart with joy and happiness, I will consider it reward enough.

—Tanushree Podder

1

What is Happiness?

Happiness is a lasting feeling of joy and gratitude. It colours our view and makes us see everything in a new light. Happiness is almost palpable, and you can certainly spot a happy person in a crowd. He stands out because of his jolly nature, optimistic mien and friendly attitude.

Happiness should not be confused with pleasure, however. Happiness is long term and innocent in nature. Unlike happiness, pleasure is short-lived and often addictive. For example, those who like to drink because of the pleasurable way in which alcohol affects their body will crave this feeling more and more. Similarly, those who seek pleasures in materialistic acquisitions soon tire of them. By itself, pleasure is not wrong but seeking pleasure as a substitute for happiness only leads to sorrow.

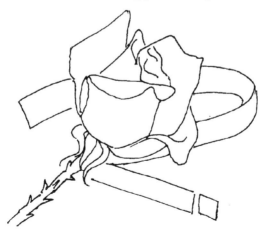

What does inner peace really mean? Are tranquillity, harmony and quietness inner peace? Can we buy inner peace? Can we learn it? Does it really exist? Almost everyone muses over these questions at some point in life. Most of us realise the need for inner peace as we progress through the different stages of life. It seems everyone – either consciously or subconsciously, directly or indirectly – is seeking this elusive goal. What is it?

In simple terms, inner peace is the peace within oneself. When we stop searching for peace externally and discover it within ourselves, we have found inner peace. This peace is not influenced by external factors. The weather, other people's behaviour, wealth or the lack of it... nothing can rob our inner peace, once it has been attained. Ultimately, inner peace is a function of one's own consciousness and is completely independent of all external input. Because of the nature of the universe, real inner peace can never be permanently found in the external world. Nature is a cycle of rotating pairs of opposites. Night follows day. Cold follows hot. Pain follows pleasure. Good times follow bad phases. Similarly, happiness follows unhappiness.

The only way to really find inner peace is to still the 'outgoing' mind and quieten the bubbling senses. Regardless of what external stimuli one can obtain, eventually one must deal with one's own restless mind. But how does one do it? It seems one has to travel a hard and long road to pursue the Utopian goal of happiness.

Wait! Don't give up even before you have begun; here is a bright ray of hope – tranquillity and happiness can be achieved with effort and practice. However, it requires consistent endeavour and will power to attain serenity of mind and soul.

2

One Simple Truth: Anyone Can Be Happy

Happiness is a wealth that knows no limits. It brings with it perfect health, joy of living and a deep sense of contentment. Do you feel it is the prerogative of certain kinds of people to be happy? I have come across many people who feel that a certain acquaintance is happier than they are: "Why should he be unhappy? He has all the money and things that can make him happy. He has a good job, social recognition, a place in society and every material thing to bring comfort; nothing is lacking."

Is it money and material things that bring happiness to an individual? Does it mean that a poor man has to be unhappy and only a rich man is happy? Nothing can be farther from the truth. I have met many people who do not have much money and don't know where their next meal will come from, yet they are happy. I have also met people who do not know what to do with their money because there is so much of it, and they are not happy. Happiness doesn't come with money; you can't buy it. In fact, the richer the person, the more his worries and the unhappier he is. I am reminded of a story that I heard as a child.

Once upon a time there lived a poor farmer who was very happy. He had no fancy garments, no possessions, just a small hut which leaked during the monsoon, a pair of coarse clothes and simple food. But he slept peacefully at night and sang throughout the day as he toiled in his field. Living nearby was a rich zamindar (landowner) with a palatial house, all material comforts to ensure a luxurious lifestyle, many servants and everything that a person could desire. Yet the rich man could not sleep at night and remained tense throughout the day. He envied the poor farmer and wanted to discover the secret of his happiness.

He went to a sage and asked him the reason for the poor farmer's happiness. The sage replied: "It is because he has no money."

"But that is impossible! How can a man be happy because he has no money? How can he sleep so blissfully at night because he has no money?" asked the rich man incredulously.

"Well, since you don't believe me, we will conduct a little test. Go and give him Rs.99 and then see the result," advised the sage.

The landowner went and gave the farmer Rs.99 as instructed by the sage. A few days later, the poor farmer came running back to him and cried: "Sir, please take this money back. I don't want it."

The rich man was surprised. "My dear man, why don't you want it? I have given it to you with all good faith. You must keep it and better your lot," he said.

"Sir, I don't want this money," the farmer insisted, "because I can't sleep peacefully any more. As long as I had no money, I could sleep in peace because I didn't have to worry about thieves stealing it. Now, I have to fix a door and lock it at night because I am worried that someone will steal the money. I also want to increase the money and have to constantly worry about how I can add another rupee and make it Rs.100. This tension is driving me mad. I can't concentrate on my work, nor sing or sleep. I don't want this money. I was happier when I didn't have it," rued the farmer.

The rich man now understood the meaning of the sage's advice. He realised that his richness was the cause of all his grief.

This is a simple story but one that holds immense truth. Money can't buy happiness. If it is not money that ensures happiness, what can do so? Have you noticed how discontentment is spreading all around us? How many people do you meet everyday who are content with their lot?

Here's an exercise! Tomorrow, ask everyone you meet if they are content and also ask them if they can name one thing they desire the most. You will be surprised by their responses. At least eight out of ten will say they are not content and begin whining about what they lack in their lives. When asked for one thing they desire, they will think very hard because there are so many things they desire!

Doesn't this illustrate how frustrated we are with our lives and how undecided we are about what we want in life?

An Exercise

Here is another exercise you could subject yourself to: list out your desires in order of priorities. You will be surprised at how difficult a task it is. Most of us do not know what we want most and are unsure about the priorities of our needs.

When I first tried this exercise, I was surprised by how quickly my mind kept changing priorities. I just couldn't decide which of my needs came first. Baffled, I pondered: What do I really want? What are my priorities? Is there any end to my wants?

I realised that the string of desires is a never-ending one. Almost every preacher, sage or spiritual guru talks about giving up desires. Right from Gautam Buddha to Jesus Christ to Guru Nanak, every saint has talked about the folly of pursuing desires. Yet we are unable to control our desires, which brings us unhappiness.

If it were not money that brings happiness, it would simply mean that every human being, rich or poor, has the ability to find happiness.

17

Does Age Matter?

I really don't think so. It has never been proved that a younger person is happier than an older one. But a child is definitely happier than an adult. Why is this so? A child is carefree and innocent; he is not bothered if his dress is more expensive than that of his friend or not. The younger the child, the happier he is.

But as the child keeps growing older, he learns the wrong things from others and unhappiness slowly seeps into his life. Yet, if he learns to be carefree and innocent like he was in childhood, happiness could still be his.

Are Men Happier Than Women?

Again, there is no proof that gender counts where happiness is concerned. There are an equal number of unhappy men and women. It simply does not matter whether you are a man or a woman where the pursuit of happiness is concerned. Of course, women are more prone to depression and depressive thoughts than men. This has much to do with their hormonal build up and moods. But, in general, happiness is not gender-specific.

If money, material things, age and sex don't matter, it simply means every human has the potential to be happy. Happiness is a natural outcome of living. Unhappiness is something we have created for ourselves through greed, excess ambition, love for material things, jealousy, competition and many other unhealthy characteristics. Most of these things increase our stress levels, leading to an unhealthy body and mind, further compounding unhappiness.

Everyone can be happy. Happiness makes no distinction between gender, class, religion or age.

◆◆◆

3

Avoid Boredom

How often we have heard everyone use the word 'bored'? Right from children to adults, all commonly use this word. A bored person is not a happy person. He is unhappy because he is unable to find any reason for amusement. A positive and busy person never gets bored. Boredom attacks inactive and indolent minds because they do not want to undertake positive activities. Boredom is also a cause of mental fatigue, which in turn leads to a feeling of constant tiredness and sluggishness. When doing something interesting, we are seldom tired. But boredom produces tiredness even when we are inactive.

When you constantly seek stimulation and excitement, whether it is physical or emotional, the search brings about frustrations repeatedly. Those who seek new excitements everyday find boredom and tedium in routine, normal living. Ask yourself: Is it possible to get exciting news everyday? If not, why shouldn't I accept the routine as a way of life and find various ways to do the same things so that I don't get bored?

There is a simple cure for boredom. Whenever I am bored and listless I put on my favourite music, don my favourite dress and tackle the chores that have been waiting for a long time. If I am feeling good, I don't get bored. And how do I feel good? The nice dress and the favourite music do the trick in making me get over my sluggishness. Why don't *you* give this cure a try? I have no doubt it will work.

Boredom is the end result for those who do not wish to make any constructive effort. ◆◆◆

4

Accept Yourself

You yourself, as much as anybody in the entire universe, deserve your love and affection.

—**Gautam Buddha**

The great Chinese philosopher, Confucius, was supposedly the most ugly boy in entire China. He had huge flapping ears, a boxer's squashed nose and sharp, protruding teeth, but he was astonishingly clever even at a very young age. As he grew older, he worked to improve the quality of life of his fellow countrymen. In time, he went on to be known as one of the wisest men in the world.

I once had a friend called Anjum. She was a great girl, pretty, intelligent and enterprising, but she suffered from a problem of her own making – she thought she was not as good as others. Each morning as she looked in the mirror she only found flaws with her looks. Either her nose was too straight or the eyebrows too close or her lips were too thick. All she saw were imperfections in her features. Anjum would often confide that she was upset at not being as good as others. She found Maneka more beautiful, Sadhana more intelligent, Rachita more good-natured, so on and so forth. When I asked her why she felt she wasn't as good as the others, she told me that God had been unfair by not giving her any good qualities.

It was a simple case of undervaluing oneself. So many people are guilty of not recognising their own talents and skills. They indulge in highlighting the missing traits and ignore the good characteristics that God gifted them. Not all of us can be as beautiful as Aishwarya Rai, yet we can highlight our plus points and come out a winner. If not beauty, most of us possess other qualities such as intelligence, a good voice, or a good hand at painting, writing or cooking. Why hanker after things we don't have? Why not concentrate and develop the attributes that we possess? It is a matter of thinking positively.

Personally, I think every woman is beautiful. If someone has good hair, the other has a lovely complexion or a fantastic bone structure. A prime example is film star Rekha. When she came into movies, she was overweight, dark and quite ordinary looking. Over a period of years, she took pains to develop her good points and turned herself into an enviable beauty.

Similarly, we have all been gifted with some talent or the other that can be honed into a winning point. I know of people who thought they were too ordinary but once they had discovered their talent and worked upon it, they became famous.

To be happy, one has to recognise the special gift given by God and feel thankful about it. Comparing oneself with others, or complaining all the time that God has been unfair, will do nothing but bring about unhappiness and discontent. When I had a long talk with Anjum, we discovered her talent with the brush. She was elated to find that she could paint commercially and today she is earning a decent sum of money through her paintings. She has also learnt not to complain about God's partiality!

In the words of Norman Vincent Peale: *"Since you have to live with yourself, it is important to develop a self that is pleasant to live with."*

Everyone has some talent; it is up to you to discover and hone it.

◆◆◆

5

Be Optimistic

Two men look out through the same bars:
One sees the mud, and one the stars.

—F Langbridge

Radha was widowed when she was just 26 years old, barely three years after her marriage. Samir died in a car crash. With a baby in the arms and little parental support, she did not have much to look forward to. But she was a survivor and an optimist. As soon as the misery had lightened, she took up a small job and set about putting her life in order. Besides the job and the baby, she also enrolled for a professional course through correspondence. We thought she was being too optimistic to think that she could cope with all these things. But she did.

Five years later, she is a leading designer and her daughter is one of the most secure children. Both have a beautiful relationship and little Riya has inherited her mother's optimistic outlook and happy nature. One feels happy meeting them because they never complain about things that have gone wrong.

Optimism is a great quality. It has many benefits. The best thing is that it never allows you to sink into the depths of depression or fatalistic thoughts. It helps you stay in good humour and look at things in bright light.

So often in life we come across people who are always complaining. Nothing ever goes well for them and they are never satisfied. Do you think such a person can be happy? Life is a cycle of ups and downs. Whatever goes up has to come down; everyone is aware of this fact. Similarly, good days will always end giving way to bad ones.

A person who is a positive thinker does not ignore the negative happenings around him; he just refuses to prolong his preoccupation with it. Positive thinking is a form of thought that habitually looks for the best results from the worst conditions. It is possible to look for something to build upon; it is possible to expect the best for yourself even though things look bad. And the remarkable fact is that when you seek good, you are very likely to find it.

How does one go about seeking the positive? Does one come across the positive just because he intends to find it? Well, it is a matter of always being positive and when one wants to find the positive in every event, even negative happenings will throw up something positive. The first step is to fill the mind with positive affirmations and crowd out negative thoughts. It is like clearing the garbage from your system. Once the garbage is cleared you will find happier thoughts filling your mind. Positive thoughts have a way of ushering in happiness within your entire being. They suffuse you with a feel-good factor that in turn brings optimism and happiness.

The most important thing to analyse is why positive thinking works. There is a definite scientific principle at work. When you fill your mind with resentment, anger and hatred, you destroy your human values and make it impossible for yourself to be at your best. Biologically, you pump in more toxins and harmful matter into your system, which ultimately harm you physically.

Sceptics declare that there is no great advantage of positive thinking. They are wrong! It definitely works if you allow it to do so. More than anything else, positivism stops you from destroying yourself. It is not an easy discipline. It takes hard work and firm belief. When the going is not good, most of us tend to give up. We don't want to hunt for the positive and easily accept the negative. The principles of positive thinking work when applied with honesty and sincerity.

Optimism is the second best thing God has given human beings; the first is the ability to remain happy. ◆◆◆

6

Turning Disadvantages into Success

The secret of success is learning how to use pain and pleasure instead of having pain and pleasure use you. If you do that, you're in control of your life.

—Anthony Robbins

Scottish inventor John Logie Baird (1888–1946) was forced to give up his business career due to illness. But he refused to let his illness tie him down and decided to work on new ideas. He moved back to Hastings, England and set up a workshop in an attic where he began experimenting with light projection. In 1925 he managed to project the image of a face from one room to the other. In 1926 he demonstrated the same at the Royal Institute of Great Britain, London. In 1937 the BBC took up his 240-line mechanically scanned system for its service. Baird didn't allow his illness to sidetrack him from his goal – and ended up pioneering television!

There is nothing that makes us unhappier than failures. It is absolutely essential that we take care of those failures and turn them around. When we are at a disadvantage, losing heart over the weakness would get us nowhere. Wise people turn their disabilities and disadvantages into advantages and transform them into success.

All of us have gone through turbulent times when nothing seems to work. This is likely to bog us down despite our best resolve. But we have an option. We can strive to turn those failures into successes. First make a list of weak points in your armour. It is generally a certain trait in our personality that plays against us, despite all efforts. For example, if you are not good at communicating with your colleagues or boss, you may have failed to present a point successfully. Once you have discovered the real reason for your failure, you are halfway to success.

Many of us tend to blame external factors for our failures. But most often, the trouble lies within us. To begin with, we have to accept those reasons. There is no point in saying the boss is unreasonable and denies you a much-deserved promotion, if you have not performed well. Analyse and improve – that should be your watchword.

If you have been able to spot chinks in the armour, it should be easy to change and mend these. If you can't do it on your own, seek professional help. For instance, if effective communication is your drawback, enrol in a workshop on communication. If you are not willing to rise above your limitations, nothing will help. Make an honest attempt. Often, we give up halfway because we don't see immediate results. The secret lies in persevering. Determination to negate your character flaws will bring about a positive change in the long run.

Here is a simple exercise that could change the way you feel about the day and its events. Decide to have a lot of fun during the day, avoid the unpleasant and seek out happy events. You will see that you feel happy and really good. After all, happiness is a state of mind. At the end of the day, you will realise that you really managed to have a great day. It began just like any other day but you managed to turn it into a happy day. Simply by thinking positive!

If you can do it for a day, can't you do it everyday? Of course, you can! Believe in it and you will be able to make a definite turnaround that will launch you into the arms of success. With success coming your way in every aspect, you will always have a happy frame of mind.

Disadvantages are simple roadblocks that people need to pass in their journey towards happiness.

◆◆◆

7

Dealing with Failures

Never mind failures; they are quite natural, they are the beauty of life – these failures; what would life be without them? It would not be worth having if it were not for struggles. So never mind these failures, these little backslidings; hold the ideal a thousand times; and if you fail a thousand times, make the attempt once more.

—**Swami Vivekananda**

Swamiji also said: "No life will be a failure; there is no such thing as failure in the universe. A hundred times man will hurt himself, a thousand times he will tumble, but in the end he will realise that he is God."

Some time ago, I was watching a TV programme 'Hero Honda Sa Re Ga Ma Pa' where the best singers are selected from amongst the participants. There was one particular participant who had won in four rounds but failed to make it in the fifth round. When the winners were announced, she couldn't stop crying. She lost all self-control and was inconsolable. Her behaviour embarrassed the organisers and other participants. Here is a person, I thought to myself, who is unable to handle failure or learn from the experience.

Failure makes most people feel helpless, at least momentarily. But some remain helpless for days or months on end even after a small setback. After major setbacks they may never recover. Who are the people who can't handle failures or view them optimistically? It is people who think about bad events in terms of 'always' and 'never'. Most of their statements begin with either of the two words: "I never win a bet" or "I always seem to lose" or "I always have trouble with my boss". Such people are permanent pessimists, which is very harmful in the long run.

On the other hand, optimistic people think in terms of 'sometimes' and 'lately'. Their statements reflect their optimism. They are likely to say: "Sometimes I am unable to perform up to optimum satisfaction" or "lately, I have been going through a rough patch", meaning these are temporary setbacks. If you use qualifiers and ascribe bad events to transient conditions, you have an optimistic style. Individuals who believe setbacks have temporary causes are more likely to recover quickly from defeat and failure.

Some people can put their troubles neatly into a compartment and go about their lives when one important aspect – say, their job or their love life – is suffering. They do not allow failure in one aspect of life to affect the other. This is a very healthy way of dealing with setbacks.

But there are others who bleed over everything. When one thread of their lives snaps, the whole fabric unravels. People who believe setbacks have specific causes are more likely to feel isolated after a defeat. Those who see causes as universal allow their defeats to undermine many areas of their life. One must understand that a setback in one area of life does not necessarily mean everything is lost.

When bad things happen we can blame ourselves (internalise) or blame others or circumstances (externalise). People who consistently blame themselves for failure suffer lower self-confidence after setbacks than people who blame external factors. Although we should take responsibility for our actions, pessimistic people often take excess responsibility for bad events.

Failures are our learning experiences. Success always follows failure, provided we have learnt from our failures.

◆◆◆

8

Focus on Your Strengths

---

*All power is within you; you can do anything. Believe in that;
do not believe that you are weak. You can do anything and
everything, even without the guidance of anyone. All power
is there. Stand up and express the divinity within you.*

—Swami Vivekananda

Often, we focus on our failures and ignore our strengths.
We want to achieve the impossible just because someone
else has managed to do it. Instead of trying to hone our
talents, we try to push ourselves on paths that are
unknown and unfamiliar. But we gain nothing except
unhappiness. If we were to exert ourselves in the strong
areas after identifying them, it would be possible to live
in peace with ourselves and attain some degree of
perfection. All this would definitely lead us to contentment
and happiness.

*Joe had a series of failures as a sales manager. He tried his best
to no avail. Finally, he consulted a career specialist. The specialist
had a long talk with Joe and made him undergo a few tests. After
the results were analysed, it was found that Joe had a very good
head for numbers and could excel in that line. It was a hard
decision for Joe to alter the course of his career but he took the risk.
After a two-year course in financial management, he took up a job
as a finance manager in the banking sector, and his career began
zooming like never before. All that Joe had needed was to spot his
particular talent and hone it.*

**In today's competitive world, focusing on strengths
marks the difference between success and failure.**

◆◆◆

Find an Inspiration

I have a friend, Raman, who has amazed me with his resilience. His life script reads like a tragedy novel. Everything that can go wrong has gone wrong in his life. Whether it is the loss of dear ones, persistent ailments or financial adversities, all kinds of depressive events have crowded Raman's life. Yet he is never depressed!

I don't know how he does it but whenever I ask him, Raman says: "Isn't life too short to spend moping around and living in self-pity? I would rather face difficulties head on." Now whenever I have a problem and feel depressed, I take a leaf out of Raman's book. Likewise, there is bound to be a similar example in your vicinity from whence you can seek inspiration.

There is always a silver lining at the end of every dark cloud. Look for that silver line and you will find it even on a stormy day. When you feel right, you tend to be joyful and look at everything in a positive light and are able to appreciate the beauty of everything around you. The mental state of a person becomes very important when he is not physically well. Those who tend to complain and remain discontented are likely to face ill health and ailments most of the time.

If you are in a good state of mind, you are likely to remain healthy and ward off most diseases. It has been proven that even those who suffer from serious ailments like cancer recover with positive thoughts and an optimistic attitude. The mind and body are inseparable. The ill health of one affects the other. When people work on their bodies to get into shape and ignore their mental and emotional well-being, they are unable to achieve hundred percent success at being fully healthy. The mind needs to be tended carefully, too.

My inspiration comes from success stories. I look up to someone who has suffered the same tragedies and actually turned them to his advantage or someone who has confronted the same faults and grown out of them. Success stories have an impelling quality and are absolutely necessary as inspirational doses. If you analyse successful people, you will realise how difficult success is. The path is full of pitfalls and rough terrain. When I read about people who got to the top despite hurdles, I find myself charged with energy and know it's possible to succeed despite all odds.

One of the most effective ways to develop self-confidence and determination is to use inspirational quotes that view life positively. Post such quotes on your wall, tape them to the mirror or recite them to yourself when required.

"When fate hands you lemons, make lemonade from them," advises Norman Vincent Peale. Yes, why not!

There is bound to be someone who can laugh at his bad luck. He is the inspiration you should seek.

◆◆◆

Mental Regimen

The will is stronger than anything else. Everything must go down before the will.

—Swami Vivekananda

Will power and perseverance are two most important ingredients of success and happiness. It is always possible to tune the mind to think strong, positive and happy thoughts.

How does one tune the mind? How can we make it think the thoughts that we know are right? This can be learnt. We often go on a diet to take charge of our physical well-being. For this, we curb our taste buds to lose weight. Similarly, we can bring about changes in our mental framework.

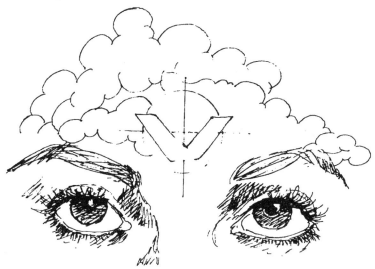

Let us try an exercise: on Monday morning, you decide you will watch every word that you utter. You will not say a single negative, mean or dishonest word. Nor say a word that could bring unhappiness to anyone, not even yourself. You will not make a depressing remark for seven days. Initially, this will not be easy. Within minutes or hours, you may say the wrong thing. But gradually, you will be able to increase the length of time during which you don't utter anything negative.

When you get to a day and then a week without negative words, it will bring about a tremendous change in your outlook. No sooner have you tested your will power for a full week, you will want to continue with the practice. Once a week elapses without faltering, you can aim for a fortnight and then a month. As time passes, the task of leashing your tongue will become so easy that speaking positive words will come naturally. Slowly and perceptibly your mental blocks will vanish and an endless stream of happy thoughts will suffuse your mind.

Physical power is not the ultimate. Mental power is. This has been demonstrated repeatedly in the stories of many survivors. Victor Frankl, author of *Man's Search for Meaning*, describes how holocaust victims used the power of their mind to survive unscathed. Although they were physically scarred, they still had the power to choose their response.

The mind is the strongest thing God has given man. Using it the right way can make all the difference between joy and sorrow, success and failure.

◆◆◆

11

Momentous Moments

Ask yourself what were the most momentous moments the previous day. When we wake up with a feeling of joy and a song on our lips, our day is likely to go well. This has something to do with the mood we wake up in. If we jump out of bed disturbed from deep sleep, we are likely to behave crankily. But if we wake up to a beautiful, sunlit morning, we are likely to feel great.

If those early moments of the day are packed with positive, joyous thoughts, your day will be full of joyful living. Similarly, at the end of the day people should feel content with the day's happenings and go to sleep with peace in their heart. A day well begun is a day full of success and joy. A day well ended is the harbinger of a peaceful night.

People who are happy and content find no difficulty in sleeping. It is only troubled minds that find sleep elusive. The degree of your happiness and contentment is reflected in your sleeping pattern. If you can fall asleep the moment your head touches the pillow, you are the happiest person on earth. But if you spend half the night tossing and turning fruitlessly, it is likely you have a lot of tensions that keep you unhappy and restless.

Tune your mind to accepting the adversities that come your way during the day and decide to turn them into advantages, everyday. You have to just decide that you will make your mind remain joyful, no matter what the situation or the circumstances. You will discover that most often you can tune your mind to such conditioning.

Can you imagine the kind of effect this simple exercise can have on your state of mind? It has a great effect not only in setting the tone for a deep and peaceful night's sleep, but also in conditioning the mind to anticipate the new day that will soon dawn. You will look forward to the new day with optimism and hope.

Think about how happy one feels when looking at a new day, watching the rising sun as the birds twitter joyously. That is the state of mind one wakes up to, but soon the entire joy is forgotten in our hurry to catch up with events that occur during the day. If we were able to constantly retain the peaceful moment, it could spread sunshine throughout the day. Basking in the sun is something but living in the shadows is quite another. You can't enjoy real fun in life if you always have your back to the sun and are pushing shadows all the time.

Every morning is a new chapter in life and every evening is the end of another chapter. Begin afresh with renewed optimism each morning.

◆◆◆

Treat People Right

A friend called Hrithik narrated his experience. He had a colleague, Sridhar, who was always trying to stab Hrithik in the back. Hrithik's happy-go-lucky disposition troubled Sridhar and the latter was forever seeking ways and means to put him down. As a result, the colleague concentrated less on his work and more on ways of displacing Hrithik from the boss's favourite list.

Hrithik, however, found this behaviour quite amusing simply because Sridhar couldn't hurt him as long as he remained unperturbed. Sridhar was only destroying himself. Throughout the drama, Hrithik never allowed Sridhar to realise that he knew what the latter was up to. He treated Sridhar with respect and helped him in his tasks. It took over six

months but gradually Sridhar began to grudgingly respect Hrithik and guilt started gnawing his mind. After a year, Sridhar's attitude towards Hrithik changed.

"I think it was insecurity that goaded the jealous behaviour," analysed Hrithik. "Basically, Sridhar is a nice person."

An important principle in leading a happy, fun-loving life is to love and respect the best in people. My father taught me a great truth: how you think about people, how you treat them and how you react to them is extremely important for your own happiness.

Most scriptures and teachings tell us that we must treat people the way we want ourselves to be treated. If we mistreat a person, no matter what his status, he is likely to return the treatment. That would hurt us, wouldn't it?

The majority act out of malice and resentment when we feel we are not being given our due. We want to mistreat the people who are not giving us enough importance. This is a sign of immaturity and childishness. It is also a very negative way of behaving. Conversely, if we treat such people with respect and deference, they are likely to be humbled. In return, they will be forced to treat us well.

When Jesus Christ said that we should turn the other cheek when a person slaps us, he was using the same logic. When you turn the other cheek, the person slapping you is likely to feel guilty and remorseful. But if you hit back, there is bound to be a spiral of violence because the process becomes unstoppable till one party bites the dust.

The best way to deal with people is to give them more respect than they deserve, simply because it prevents them from acting obnoxiously.

One good turn begets another.

◆◆◆

13

Give Till You Ache

It is more blessed to give than to receive.

—New Testament, Acts, XX, 35

According to Mother Teresa, giving away what we don't require is not charity. Charity is when we give away what we need most. Giving away what makes your heart ache, in simple terms, is charity. Have you ever experienced the happiness that giving brings?

The joy of giving is immeasurable. Giving does not necessarily mean giving money. You could give your time or help or advice – in fact, you could give anything that costs something to you and can help others. It's a strange principle but it's true, nevertheless, that those who give the most have the most of whatever they give.

It is said that God returns manifold what you give away. There are so many instances of people who found their meagre resources growing after they had shared it with the needy. Many people I meet tell me that they don't have enough to give away. This is not true. Everyone has enough to share, it is just that we are greedy and want to keep it all with us.

Just think – if we put away only 50 paise everyday for charity, it would amount to Rs.15 in a month and Rs.180 per year. That would be enough to buy notebooks for a needy child who is interested in studying or buy clothes for someone. Most of us can afford to put away fifty paise, can't we?

It isn't essential we give Rs.500 for charity. Sometimes, just Rs.5 to buy a meal for a hungry person is enough to bring about a sense of satisfaction and joy in our and the recipient's lives. Remember, you are not doing charity for someone else by giving them food or clothes. It is a favour you are doing yourself by making life more meaningful for you.

We all come into this world without any riches or possessions and leave the world empty-handed. Then why should we hoard material possessions throughout our life and bring ourselves so much unhappiness and tension. If we learn to live life in simple terms without any greed for material things, we are likely to remain content and happy.

Charity ensures joy.

◆◆◆

This is Life

Life is an adventure; venture into it,
Life is a journey; complete it,
Life is a path full of roses and thorns,
Enjoy the roses and pick out the thorns.

There is no one in the world who does not have his share of troubles and anxieties. When we go through adversities in life, we always assume that God has singled us out for unfair treatment. In our ignorance, we feel that we are encountering more distressful events than others. We forget the months of happiness and success we have enjoyed.

Anxieties are caused by our way of interpreting events. If we can interpret it in a positive manner we could use the experience to learn and grow, but if we interpret the same in a negative way, we will feel defeated by the event. The power of positive thinking can help us overcome adversity with ease, while the negative attitude can rob us of our happiness, self-esteem and optimism.

When Prashant was unable to get admission in IIT despite full preparation, he didn't lose hope. He applied at the Regional Engineering College and got admission. After that he continued to work hard and passed out with flying colours. He was picked up by an MNC in a campus interview and his life was made.

Positive minds think differently. When a door closes they expect many windows to open. This makes all the difference.

Just as every dawn is followed by dusk, happiness and joy are followed by sorrow. It is how you accept this cycle that ensures peace.

◆◆◆

15

Why Me?

Most of us ask this question whenever calamity hits us. If a loved one dies, we lose our job, lose money or if anything disturbing happens, we ask this question over and again.

When overcome with grief, instead of wondering 'Why me?' think of others going through similar experiences and reach out to them. It will deepen your sense of compassion and empathy for people in similar situations.

Sometime ago, Satish lost his legs in an accident. He was distraught and depressed for a long time till he suddenly realised that he could help others in a similar predicament. He began an association for people who had lost their limbs. The association counselled and helped such people and soon Satish found a purpose in life. Instead of wallowing in self-pity, he found an outlet for his energies in a positive manner.

When Mumbai was ravaged by bomb explosions or when the dreaded SARS hit people in many countries, it was a devastating experience for most families. For the people who lost a loved one or more family members, there was no light at the end of the tunnel. Life seemed totally bleak and hopeless. Yet, people lived through the tragedy and life went on. Many regained their happy disposition after a while because time is the greatest healer.

It's easy to focus on the sufferings caused by tragic events. But instead of asking 'Why me?' ask 'Why not me?' This little query will help you maintain a positive outlook during your period of trial and tribulations.

Learning to accept tough times helps us live through them with peace and equanimity.

◆◆◆

A Matter of Attitude

Two friends were walking in the park. Just as they turned a corner, dark and threatening clouds covered the skies and soon a torrent of heavy showers compelled them to seek cover under a tree. One of them remarked: "There goes our walk. Why did it have to start raining just now?"

The other said: "It is so beautiful. I could stand here the entire day, watching the rain fall on the parched earth, giving it a new lease of life. Look at the leaves and flowers, they almost seem to be singing with joy at the advent of the monsoon showers after a long dry spell."

The contrasting attitude between the two friends is as stark as day and night. While one rejoiced when it rained, the other grumbled. Basically, it is a matter of attitude. Almost every event can be viewed in two different ways: positive or negative. While the positive attitude helps us coast along with pleasure, the negative attitude can make us cynical, pessimistic individuals.

We are bombarded by negative messages – television, radio, print media, the Internet, all carry messages of death, destruction and tragedy. In fact, everything bad that one can imagine seems to be happening all around. Through all this, how can we stay positive? Is it possible? And if we maintain a positive outlook, are we just seeing the world through the proverbial rose-tinted glasses?

There is a difference between blindly ignoring reality and acknowledging reality but still picking out the positives. The world can be a cruel place because there is crime, unhappiness and disease. The world can also be a wonderful place because there is love, compassion and joy. Both scenarios exist side by side and will affect us throughout our lives. But how we choose to view the world can make the difference between being happy or unhappy. Quite honestly, attitude is the deciding factor. It is the crucial difference between optimism and pessimism. It is the difference between two contrasting opinions: the glass is half-full or half-empty. For an optimistic person, there are no barriers – everything swings on well-oiled hinges.

A positive attitude makes all the difference. Learning to take the highs with the lows helps during rough weather.

◆◆◆

How to Remain Positive

Fyodor Mikhailovich Dostoevsky, the famous Russian novelist (1821–1881), led an eventful life fraught with danger. Some of his books – Crime and Punishment, The Idiot, The Brothers Karamazov – *are considered classics. Dostoevsky spent a significant part of his youth in the army before he took up writing. At one stage, he got involved in a plot against the government. But he was caught and a court sentenced him to death. Luckily, his death sentence was commuted to a spell of imprisonment in Siberia.*

Eventually he was released and when he returned to European Russia he began a magazine called The Times. *His magazine was very critical of the government and Dostoevsky was forced to close it down. Several times thereafter, he tried to re-establish the magazine but didn't succeed. Instead, he slid into debt and had to leave the country.*

Despite repeated setbacks, he was a born optimist who found something positive in every situation. Neither his death sentence nor imprisonment in Siberia nor the forced closure of his magazine could rob him of his positive mindset and he continued to pen his novels, which ultimately made him world famous.

Is it easy to maintain a positive attitude at all times? No, it isn't! Despite our best resolutions, we are likely to falter on the path of positivism. Philosophers tell us to treat the reverses in our life as learning experiences. But what happens when a "learning experience" ruins our lives? How many persevere and continue on the enlightened path. Most of us want to lead our lives according to situational demands. And this path is definitely not enlightened! Hardships become a learning experience only when we view them objectively and remain detached from the results.

When a major negative happens, perhaps the death of a loved one, or being victimised by a crime such as rape or murder, being "enlightened" and viewing the events as another learning experience is difficult. We try to do so – sometimes we succeed and at other times we fail.

Failing is human! Negative things will continue to affect us; no one lives a charmed life. At such times we are likely to view the event in a mostly negative light. By the same token, positive things will also occur. But the difference between a positive and a negative mindset lies in the fact that the positive mindset will allow one to emphasise the good and ignore the bad. You can pick the good out of a bad situation because no situation is totally bad.

By having a positive outlook, we are not ignoring reality or denying our emotions. Being positive does not mean you have to make a superhuman effort and hold back your tears or become unfeeling even when tragedy strikes you; it simply means we should not allow ourselves to be trapped in a rut and dwell endlessly on the reverses. Being positive implies allowing ourselves time to heal and then moving forward.

Making a new life and rising above adversities is what positive thinking is all about. Ask yourself: "So what?" each time you are hit and bounce back really hard. "What is the worst thing that can happen?" Ask yourself that and you'll find that most of the time we exaggerate bad situations. The truth is that if we were to balance the ledgers of our lives, we will discover that the sum of negatives will always be outweighed by all the positives.

Life is about finding little pieces of joy in bundles of adversity.

◆◆◆

Attitudinal Tuning

When I was a child, I had a very irritating habit of asking too many questions. Most children do the same. But when we become adults, we are scared to ask questions or maybe we are too conscious about our status in society and other factors. So we stop asking questions.

What happens when we stop asking questions? We receive no answers!· The same thing applies to the text that goes under the word 'attitude'. We never stop and ask ourselves why we harbour certain negative attitudes. Is it so difficult to change an attitude?

Just ask yourself these questions and then implement an adjustment in your attitude for just two incidents every day. Each time you find negative thoughts crowding your mind, just say: "I am going to banish this wrong attitude and think the right way." Force yourself to substitute the wrong attitude with the right one. After a few months, you will be surprised at how easy the task becomes. It is as easy as switching channels on your television!

The right attitude can land a person a job, and also ensure a good relationship, a sense of happiness and everything else, while the wrong attitude can destroy all these and more. To cultivate the right attitude, you must tune your thoughts like you would tune your favourite television channel to receive a clearer picture. The mind can also be tuned to think in a certain manner. It can be programmed to think positively in almost any situation.

As we begin afresh each day, we have an option to tune our minds in a negative mode or strike out on a positive note. Negative thinking will bring a sense of insecurity and cynicism, thereby affecting our progress and well-being, while positive thoughts will usher a sense of peace and well-being. No one can expect ideal conditions throughout life because we live in a world of imperfection and adversities. But it is within our power to turn those adverse situations into positive outcomes.

Each day you have an option: wallow in unhappiness or bask in the sunshine of positive thoughts and happiness.

Switch on the Smile

It's easy enough to be pleasant,
When life flows along like a song;
But the man worthwhile is the one who will smile
When everything goes dead wrong.

—Ella Wheeler Wilcox

We have all heard about the saying that a smile stretches for a mile. We have also heard how a smile begets a smile and makes strangers warm up to us. Volumes have been written about the benefits of a smile: it lights up the eyes, imparts colour to the cheeks and brings so many facial muscles into play, exercising them thoroughly. A smile also promotes good health and improves the complexion. It diffuses stress, improves relationships and controls situations that threaten to go out of hand. It releases feel-good hormones in our system... One can go on and on about all the good one little smile does. So many benefits in one little expression of joy.

So what prevents you from switching on a thousand-watt smile every morning? It may sound foolish when I suggest that you should smile at strangers – but it works! Try it out, if you don't believe me. Here is an exercise for the day. Tomorrow morning, wake up with a smile on your face. First smile at your reflection in the bathroom mirror as you brush your teeth. Then smile at all family members when you say "Good morning!" Smile broadly and dazzle people on the road as you drive to work. Nod and smile at the traffic cop when he waves you through. Again, switch on the smile as you enter the lift and the office.

It works like magic. At least 70% people will return your smile, barring a few preoccupied ones. You will feel your heart singing and the soul lifting as they smile back at you. You will feel the warmth of sunshine and joy spreading through your body with each smile. You will make new friends who will smile back when they see you again. Imagine being greeted by smiles on a day when you aren't feeling too bright! Won't that lift the dark clouds from your mind and bring the bliss surging back?

A smile has a way of communicating happy thoughts more than words can. It is infectious because everyone catches it. It is magical because it makes you feel good. And you look beautiful with a smile on your face, unlike when you are grouchy or serious. A smile gets the happy hormones flowing in your body that do wonders for your health. It also leaves a lasting impression on people, who say: "There goes a happy soul. God bless him!"

You must have heard the riddle: "What stretches for a mile?" Smiles, of course! Still need more reasons to usher in the day with a smile?

A simple smile can light up your life and bring joy to everyone around you.

◆◆◆

Get a Grip Over Your Mood

We have heard it so often – people complaining that they are not in a mood to do something or that their mood is so foul they don't even feel like talking. What are moods? Moods are something that foul up the day – yours and everyone else's. They are excuses people use when they don't want to do something.

There are times when film stars complain they don't want to shoot a scene because they are not in the mood to do so. Do they care about the fact that the producer is spending several lakhs of rupees on the sets and for wages or that the time of other workers is equally precious? All they care about is their own mood. A professional must not be dictated by mood swings. Can a doctor refuse to perform a lifesaving surgery just because he is not in the mood? Can a bus driver refuse to drive because he is not in the mood to do so? Can a factory worker stop production because he is not in the mood? Never!

Should we let moods dictate our life or should we dictate our moods? The question needs no answer. We can never let our moods come in the way of our normal functioning. We would only be adding to our woes if we did so. Make a wilful effort to improve your mood and you'll find it works.

We should control our moods instead of allowing them to control us.

Control Your Emotions...

The difference between the great man who is emotional and the failure who is also emotional is that the great man takes care of his emotions and knows how to use them while the failure does not.

We are all slaves of our emotions. But emotions need not be a handicap. In fact, they can be valuable assets when used in the right manner. Emotional people tend to be moody and moods lead to a lot of unpleasantness and unhappiness. They affect not just one individual but everyone around them too. Positive emotions are love, peace and harmonious thinking. Negative ones are anger, jealousy and resentment. Emotional people rarely succeed. That is not to say that good emotions like kindness, respect, love, generosity etc should be kept in check. These are emotions that will help us grow into better human beings and shape our personalities in a positive manner. But here we are referring to negative emotions that can alter the way we behave significantly, mostly negatively.

Emotional people experience more misery and depression than those who can keep their emotions in check. Anger is one of the most destructive emotions and can cause high blood pressure and depression. Not expressing your anger can create other problems as well. It may cause you to display passive aggressive behaviours, or to constantly act grumpy, moody or cynical.

Most of us allow our emotions to be governed by outside influences, if not directly, then indirectly. The way you interpret the world ultimately determines how you feel. You may believe that how you perceive the world is

not in your control, but every situation affords many possible interpretations. Your interpretation of an event depends on your attitude. You may tend to focus on the negative and anticipate the worst, because you believe it serves a purpose, perhaps to prepare or protect you. Most often, however, our negative interpretations hurt rather than protect us.

Although it is important to heed our feelings, they are not necessarily an accurate reflection of reality all the time. Yet, emotions are signals from the mind and body. They draw your attention to things that are damaging you. They pull you towards things that will help you. In this sense, emotions should be analysed and heeded. However, we should know when to follow our emotions and when to control them.

Equanimity can often help us ride smoothly over the ups and downs in life.

◆◆◆

...But Don't Repress Them

Suppressed emotions can explode like a volcano someday, causing great emotional and physical harm. About 70% of our physical ailments are caused due to suppressed emotions, which eat away into our mind and body.

New age guru Deepak Chopra says we suppress emotions to protect ourselves from being hurt. "However, the resistance to feeling your emotions when they arise is what really causes pain. Unfelt and unexpressed emotions manifest in many ways. They may be felt only on a discomfort level, as if something is wrong and you don't know what it is. Sometimes it's even hard to pinpoint what exactly is the cause of your disease or discomfort... Sometimes it's a feeling of anger or disappointment that doesn't seem to have a cause," he opines.

But suppressed emotions are likely to cause greater harm to others and to us when they explode at some point of time. This is exactly like the pressure weight on your cooker, which will finally explode if you don't allow it to ventilate.

Pent-up emotions cause a lot of unhappiness and high stress levels are directly linked to suppressed emotions. When we try to keep the feelings bottled up within, we are creating a whole gamut of problems. Whether negative or positive, emotions need to be expressed. You will not be human if you do not have feelings and it would be unnatural if you keep suppressing them. Therefore, find ways and means of expressing your emotions safely.

An easy and calm mind can only be attained when emotions are allowed safe expression.

◆◆◆

Seek Good, Ignore Shortcomings

One of the major tendencies of all human beings is that they seek perfection. But there is nothing like a perfect human being or thing in this world. When we ourselves are not perfect, how can we seek perfection in others? Every human being has some good and some bad traits. That's how God has programmed us. We try to become better persons yet we are never perfect.

If we are constantly chiding our loved ones for their imperfection and finding fault in them, there is bound to be unpleasantness around us. Unpleasantness creates tension and unhappiness. So what is the way out?

We are most unhappy when our relationships are going through rough weather. If we were to curb our criticism of others, we could definitely have a better relationship with everyone around us. When we are looking for faults, our eyes focus on the negative qualities of others and we derive great pleasure in telling them what is wrong with them. When we fight with our spouses we love to tell them about the time they were wrong, we try to win arguments by pinpointing their inadequacies.

But we forget that they have their virtues and still possess many endearing qualities because of which we married them. Yet we highlight the shortcomings rather than focus on the ·strengths.

Whether at the workplace or home, constant nitpicking can create much unhappiness and turmoil, which in turn creates an unhappy situation for us. If faultfinding could ensure happiness even for a single person, fine. But it only promotes unhappiness. So why find faults?

Just ponder for a moment: what would happen if the scenario was reversed and we looked only for the good in everything and everyone.

Recall the story of Akbar and Birbal, where the latter always said: "Whatever happens, happens for the best." He was naive enough to say the same thing when the Akbar injured his finger while on a hunt. The king was furious and ordered that Birbal be jailed. A short while later, Akbar was captured by some tantriks who wanted to sacrifice him to Goddess Kali. But when they noticed that he was injured, they decided against it because the Goddess would not accept the sacrifice of a man who was not perfectly healthy. The injury saved Akbar's life and opened his eyes. He ordered that Birbal be set free immediately.

But Akbar inquired about what good it did Birbal since he was thrown into prison. Birbal responded that had he been with the king during his capture, the tantriks would surely have sacrificed him in place of Akbar, since he was in the pink of health. Being thrown into prison saved his life.

The moral of the story is that a good point can always be found in the worst situations if we look closely. Likewise, instead of spending time finding faults, we should seek out the goodness in others. You will then discover happiness everyday.

There is good in everyone. It is for us to recognise the positive aspect in people.

◆◆◆

Accept What You Can't Change

Most of us are unhappy because we want something or someone to change to suit our needs. We want our spouses, children, friends, colleagues, workplace, home and the world to change so that they suit the image we have in mind. In our minds, we have an image to suit every relationship and circumstance. If the person does not fit the bill, we are unhappy. But instead of trying to change everything and everyone around us, wouldn't it be far easier to mould ourselves to fit into the world?

It relieves me to accept things I cannot change. It is far easier to accept consequences, and to accept fundamental facts about the world and existence.

Acceptance is an expression of power. If I have already done all that I can do, I can relax and choose to let it go, because I have that power.

Most of us can't change the situations around us. If we are working in a specific job, we have to make do with it. It is not possible to change the job or expect colleagues to change. Accepting the fact that these are unchangeable makes it easier for us to adjust with circumstances. The process of adjustment becomes far easier when one accepts the hard truth that we cannot change things around us. It is better to mould ourselves to suit the situation than trying to change everything and ending up frustrated.

Frustrations occur when we find ourselves struggling against repeated failures. Failure results when we can't change things. We find ourselves getting angry and frustrated simply because we can't get along with our colleagues or the boss. But ask yourself for a moment: why should I expect them to change when I can't change myself?

Sometime ago, I was reading a book by Debbie Ford where she asks: "How would our lives alter if we saw our co-workers as divine beings come to impart essential wisdom to us? What would happen if we listened to our neighbours as though they were the wisest people in the world? And what would be possible if we related to our partners as though their sole purpose was to bring us ecstasy and joy?"

These are pertinent questions. If one is able to answer them honestly and implement these in daily life, the result would a very happy life.

Accepting the inevitable makes it easier to remain happy.

◆◆◆

There Are No Shortcuts

Most people can never accept that there are no shortcuts in life. Whether it is money, status, success, popularity or even happiness, we want everything to happen with the wave of a magic wand. This is not possible. It is only persistent efforts that can help us realise our goals. There are no shortcuts to anything. Consider the late Dhirubhai Ambani. The Rs.65,000-crore Reliance Group did not materialise in a matter of months or a few years. It took a few decades of persistent hard work for a man who began life so humbly to reach the skies. We want to replicate the success of Ambani without undergoing the pains, frustrations and disappointments that he went through.

Amitabh Bachchan also did not become an internationally acclaimed actor easily. There was a time when the lanky, dark and not-so-handsome actor was rejected by many producers and directors in Bollywood. Bachchan had a series of flops but was determined to succeed. If he later made history, it was only because of his persistence, perseverance and self-belief.

Can we put in the same efforts to succeed? Not only are we averse to this, we also set unrealistic goals and then fret when we can't achieve them. A slow-and-steady progress based on realistic goals would be a more practical approach. The joy of success can be tasted when we set achievable targets and work steadily towards them.

The path to success is a long one and there are no shortcuts to the goal.

◆◆◆

26

I Want More, Right Now!

We always want something or the other. The moment we spot something new in a shop, we want it. Not because we need it but because our friend or neighbour has it. If we have a scooter, we want a car. We are happy for sometime after we buy the car but this happiness does not last long. A few years later, we want a better, bigger, sleeker car. We see a friend travelling in an air-conditioned car and we are envious because our car is not air-conditioned. Suddenly, acquiring a car air-conditioner becomes a priority. We struggle to raise the money for months, cutting corners, working harder and dreaming of nothing else until we manage to buy the coveted air-conditioner. We should be happy now! But are we happy?

Yes! For a few days or weeks we feel elated showing off our new acquisition and talking about it. But gradually the novelty wears off... Suddenly, our eyes settle on a new home theatre with novel features and high fidelity. Now that becomes the latest object of our desire! The cycle of yearning for it, saving for it, acquiring it, talking about it, enjoying it and then getting bored of it begins anew!

But should we be perpetual slaves to our desires? There will always be new products in the market and aggressive advertising aimed at stoking our desires will always exist. Shops will keep displaying their wares attractively since they need buyers. But how long will I be able to compete with my neighbour and for how long will my purse oblige? My dissatisfaction and frustration will increase each time I am unable to buy what I desire. Sometimes, I may resort to unethical means to raise the funds required to keep pace with my desires. Will I sleep peacefully after that?

If I am unable to come to terms and live peacefully after I commit a dishonest act, then is it worth the effort? Is material acquisition more important than peace of mind? Recently, I read a book that contained a beautiful thought: *appreciate a thing of beauty without desiring it.* Such a profound thought in one simple sentence. An artist is able to appreciate the beauty of a flower or a woman without trying to possess the same. It is this distinction in attitude that is critical. If you are able to appreciate the new car in the showroom and walk away without the nagging desire to possess it, you have overcome your desires. Simultaneously, you are calm and content because you don't have the aching desire to buy it.

Even if you do have a legitimate desire, you need to consider a time frame and not seek to have it fulfilled immediately. When the time is ripe your desire will be fulfilled, after you have earned enough money through hard work. But most of us want everything immediately. A doctor just out of medical college wants to have a roaring practice, which will bankroll all his desires. So what does he do? He begins to fleece every patient, regardless of whether the patient can afford it or not. He forsakes the Hippocratic Oath at the altar of commercialism. All humanity vanishes from his nature because money becomes the driving force. He does not want to wait till his practice has stabilised and he can afford the little luxuries of life.

Years later, when he is old, wizened and stooped with age, will he be able to live with the haunting thought of having duped thousands of patients, many of them poor people? Will his soul not reproach him for all his wrongs? Will he ever rest in peace?

Basing our happiness upon material achievements will only make us unhappy.

◆◆◆

27

Forgive and Forget

He who is devoid of the power to forgive is devoid of the power to love.

—Dr Martin Luther King, Jr

According to famous motivational author Stephen Covey: "When you forgive, you open the channels for trust and unconditional love. You clean your heart. You also remove a major obstacle that keeps others from changing – because when you don't forgive, you put yourself between people and their conscience. Instead of spending energy on work with their own conscience, they spend it defending and justifying their behaviour to you."

Old resentments and failed expectations often interfere with the enjoyment of our lives – try to identify the pain and then move on. Forgiveness is letting go of the need for revenge and releasing negative thoughts of bitterness and resentment. If you are a parent, you can be a wonderful model for your children by forgiving. If they observe your reconciliation with those who have wronged you, they will also learn not to harbour resentment.

Here are some easy steps towards forgiveness:
- Acknowledge your own inner pain.
- Express your emotions in non-hurtful ways without yelling or attacking.
- Protect yourself from further victimisation.
- Try to understand the point of view of the person to be forgiven; replace anger with compassion.
- Forgive yourself for your role in a difficult relationship, and then decide whether or not to remain in the relationship.

- Perform the overt act of forgiveness verbally or in writing. If the person you want to forgive is dead or unreachable, you can still write down your feelings in the form of a letter.

It happened many years ago. I was struggling to create a niche as a writer and making an all-out effort to reach my goal. During that time I met a friend who had studied with me in college. She was working for a newspaper as a trainee sub-editor. I asked if it was possible for me to get something published in the newspaper she worked for. Her response: "It is not possible for everyone to become a writer. A writer has to be born with certain traits and qualities."

I was taken aback. Her remarks made me more determined than ever and I continued my struggle. Two years later, I had become an established writer through sheer grit and hard work. When I met my friend again, I thanked her for making me a writer. She was shocked. Instead of rebuking her and seeking revenge I was thanking her and she couldn't believe it. "Had you not spoken those words, I would never have steeled myself to make the extra effort that finally made it possible for me to succeed," I told her.

Our friendship took a new turn and the relationship grew better after that.

For a minute, imagine the result if I had lambasted her, or been sarcastic or hated her. I would have lost a good friend. I could have let her words depress me. But what would I have achieved if I did that? When we harbour unforgiveness in our hearts we suffer – immensely. It is wiser to let go of the negative feelings so that we can remain happy.

Most of us love to take revenge. Hardly do we perceive some slight from a person and we want to give it back. But thoughts of revenge can harm our emotional and physical self, causing us much agony. Forgiveness and compassion are better than being vengeful and judgmental. It takes a lot of strength to be compassionate and very little to be judgmental. But the beauty is that anyone can learn to be compassionate with a little effort.

Here are some truths about forgiveness:

- Many of us want to forgive. We know from experience that forgiving feels better than hating and hurting. We want to express our generosity and compassion. But we don't really understand what forgiveness is all about.
- We often tell ourselves 'I should only forgive if they apologise'. Without apology, contrition, reparations, promises of reform, or at least some guarantee of sincerity on the part of the wrongdoer, it's tough to forgive. We wait for the wrongdoer to do something right for a change. It may not be that way. So learn to forgive without any apology.
- Keep the doors to your heart open. Here's the best part: When you forgive, your heart opens. Then you have an open heart, instead of a clenched fist where your heart belongs.
- Let positive energy cleanse it. Be large-hearted and magnanimous. Forgiveness is empowering.
- Many of us believe that our own happiness cannot be achieved until someone comes crawling to us on hands and knees, or learns their lesson, or promises to be different. But our happiness is not really dependent upon the behaviour of other people. The forgiver changes her focus from "if only they would" to "I wonder if I could..."
- Forgiveness is a skill. It becomes a way of life when you practise it constantly.

Forgive even if there is no apology from the wrongdoer. Forgiveness ensures peace of mind.

◆◆◆

Be Humble and Generous

Isaac Newton was one of the finest and most respected scientists Britain has ever produced. He was educated at Grantham Grammar School and completed his BA at Trinity College, Cambridge. One day, as a young physicist, Newton observed that when apples fell off trees they went down at a speed that varied according to the distance they had to travel to the ground. He believed that this meant the earth had a gravitational force pulling them down, and thus his theory of gravity was born. He applied this principle to the movement of the planets and stars in the solar system. He then began to study the heavens closely. This led to the discovery of the composition of light.

There were many other original ideas evolved and developed by Newton, including the famous Laws of Motion, and the differential calculus that are the foundation of the science of mechanics today. During his lifetime, Newton was greatly respected everywhere not only for his astonishing gifts as a scientist and thinker, but also for the modesty with which he demonstrated them, and the kindliness he showed to everyone who came his way. Nothing was too much trouble. He never displayed impatience with those less intelligent than himself.

Humility is a virtue that few possess. We all want to flaunt our power, our knowledge and our wealth. We want to show that we are better than others. If someone belittles us, we feel humiliated and think: "How could he treat me like that? Doesn't he know that I am so and so?" What is it that makes us unable to act normal and pleasant?

It is our ego. An inflated ego will never allow a person to behave normally. He will succumb to unhappiness if he feels others are not treating him with due respect. There is an ancient Sanskrit saying which says that the tree laden with fruits is likely to stoop while the one without any fruits will remain tall and rigid. Similarly, a person without knowledge is filled with false pride while the truly learned will be humble. The latter are spiritual in nature and not slaves to base things like pride and vanity.

Pride and vanity often come in the way of happiness simply because happiness requires a degree of humility, detachment and contentment with one's lot.

I have often come across people who espouse their humility: "I am a humble person." Can such people really be humble? A humble person does not go around proclaiming this fact! He who is truly humble does not speak about it.

True humility is a great virtue that can bring unlimited joy in life.

Stop Nitpicking

This is one of the habits that most of us enjoy. Gossip, nitpicking, criticising and shredding someone's reputation to pieces. At a party, you are likely to find groups of people who enjoy nothing better than maligning others. Malicious gossip gives them immense pleasure. At work, home or elsewhere, such people revel in finding faults in everything and everyone. Who is perfect? No one! Then what right do we have to criticise everyone?

It is easier to grow close to someone when neither person spends time judging the other. Being judged all the time makes it impossible to share. Sometimes it is difficult to visualise the good in a person or a situation because they look thoroughly bad. But there is always a good side to everything and everyone; it is for us to spot it.

Blaming the government, an organisation or our company is of no use if we, as individuals, contribute nothing towards making a change in the system. We have the duty to change things for the better, instead of nitpicking or blaming the system. While we blame others, there will always be others doing the same about us.

A famous Zen thought is: *What goes around comes around.* Whatever negative vibrations you throw into the atmosphere will eventually find their way to you.

Blame no one for your situation. If things are bad, you must make the effort to improve them.

Nothing is Permanent

Whether it's life itself or one's health, money or success, nothing is everlasting. Then why should we chase impermanent things and become unhappy when we cannot acquire them. Even relationships are impermanent. We have all come empty-handed and will leave this world empty-handed; all the material things we acquire will remain here. Once this philosophy is truly understood it is easy to lead a life of peace and contentment.

After the Gujarat earthquake, I met several Gujarati businessmen who had been very rich before the quake. They had every material comfort but were now starting afresh because they had lost everything. This encounter made me ponder. We sweat day and night to accumulate money, lose our sleep over petty matters and suffer so much, for what? Is money and wealth really worth all the trouble it takes to acquire it? Is it more important than the peace of mind and happiness that a carefree and hassle-free life can give us?

Pause for a moment and think – if nothing is permanent, can problems be permanent? That is another point to ponder about. No problem can be permanent nor can a bad phase last long. This alone should be enough to cheer us up.

Money and success have no permanence. Why make ourselves unhappy or stressed out chasing them!

◆◆◆

Learn to Laugh at Problems

A merry heart maketh a cheerful countenance.

—Old Testament, Proverbs, XV, 13

The power of humour is a strong one. The ability to laugh away problems is a quality that can see one through all the low phases of life. Humour is a powerful distraction, no matter how worried or distraught one is. Most of our problems are really trivial and temporary. We blow them out of proportion and give them undue importance. A small loss in the share market or a monetary setback is not important enough for us to lose sleep over. If we are strong, healthy and have a happy frame of mind, we will be able to recoup any losses.

What matters is the ability to take things in our stride. We can get over the seriousness of any setback if we can see the lighter side. The worst tensions can dissolve when one is able to laugh at the situation. Strained relationships, troubled situations, anything and everything can benefit from a sense of humour.

One of the most brilliant comedians of all time, Charlie Chaplin suffered immense misery as a child. His father was a drunkard and his mother was a singer and dancer mostly out of work. Mother and children suffered periods of intense hardship and poverty. Charlie made his debut in a music hall when he was five and was quite a seasoned performer by the age of eight.

In 1914, he went to Hollywood, where the film industry was just coming into being. He brought the tragic experience of his life to stage and gave it a comical twist. Audiences laughed and wept at the tiny, downtrodden figure with the bowler hat, cane, moustache and turned-out feet, which was the early, most brilliant Charlie Chaplin. He made 35 films in one year. The tramp he created became a rage. Charlie Chaplin, who was knighted in 1975, learned to laugh at his problems and created his huge success on the foundation of his tragic childhood.

A good laugh relaxes the mind, exercises facial muscles, reduces blood pressure and improves circulation. Laughing heartily is one of the best ways of overcoming frustrations and tensions of modern existence. Develop a sense of humour and it will work wonders for you and your family. Break into laughter and see the tension dissolve all around you.

Laughter is infectious – spread it around generously.

◆◆◆

Every Problem has a Solution

Success is how high you bounce when you hit the bottom.

—General George Patton

We have all heard stories of Akbar and Birbal. It is said that Birbal had a solution for every problem that troubled the great emperor. Birbal had one of the quickest minds in the world and his quick wit was heavily laced with humour.

If Birbal could do it, so can you. The trick is to realise that there is no problem in this world that cannot be solved or no tragedy that doesn't end. Most of us lose hope and cry in frustration rather than fight back and seek solutions. Has any problem seemed insurmountable to you? Yet, for how long did it last? Finally, you would have found a way around it. Whatever your approach, the problem didn't kill you! We get caught in our own web of problems because we brood and worry instead of finding answers.

The beauty of life is its unpredictable nature. There would be no fun in living if there were no ups and downs. The regular challenges make life more interesting. To give up and cry is not the way to handle situations that demand our intelligence. Sometimes the solution is so simple that we kick ourselves for not having thought about it earlier!

The great scientist Galileo Galilei's life illustrates the fact that adversities should be accepted so that one can move ahead with life. Around 1580, when he was a student in Pisa, Galileo sat watching a candelabrum in the Pisa Cathedral swing on a rope from side to side. After a while he noticed that the swing took the same time from left to right, although the distance was getting shorter. He had discovered that pendulum movement produces a regular time measurement and from this observation he developed the theory of specific gravity.

Galileo became professor of mathematics at Padua, and in his time he put forward many revolutionary ideas. He showed that in a vacuum bodies of different weights fall to the ground at the same speed. He invented the astronomical telescope and with it proved that Copernicus' theory was correct.

Like many contemporary scientists, Galileo faced many problems because of his revolutiȯnary ideas. Churches in those times wielded enormous power and were at loggerheads with many inventors and scientists. They compelled Galileo to withdraw statements regarding his scientific observations. The brilliant man complied with their dictates in the interests of science, so that he could continue working. Galileo discovered many beneficial theories for the betterment of the human race.

Had Galileo been depressed after being asked to negate his theories or inventions, many of his later efforts would never have seen the light of day.

It is better to seek solutions instead of crying over the problems in life.

Time is the Greatest Healer

Although the world is full of suffering, it is full also of the overcoming of it.

—Helen Keller

Truer words were never spoken. When we languish in self-pity and nurse our miseries, we fail to lead a normal life. Sufferings are touchstones that should purify us and give us fresh impetus to get on with the business of living.

Madame Curie is the only person ever to win two Nobel prizes. It is a rare honour and more so because she was a woman. She and her husband Pierre were research graduates in Paris towards the end of the nineteenth century, working in the exciting new field of X-rays and looking for elements that gave off these valuable rays. After years of patient experiments they finally isolated radium, and the discovery brought them tremendous fame. The couple won the Nobel Prize for physics in 1903.

Pierre Curie was killed in a tragic road accident three years after winning the prize, leaving Marie Curie to carry on the good work they had begun. Although heartbroken, Madame Curie carried on her research work, and the University of Paris made her professor of physics. In 1911, she won her second Nobel Prize. Radium has a wide range of uses, especially in medicine. Cancer patients the world over have much to thank Madame Curie for. Her discovery has been extensively used to combat cancer.

Imagine, if Marie Curie had given up her research and wallowed in grief and self-pity, would the world have benefited from her discovery? She took the grief in her stride and although she missed her life partner and research mate, she carried on with her mission. If Marie Curie could do it, so can each of us. We all suffer grief at some time or the other. But should we allow our sorrows to stop life's clock? No! The show must go on!

Sometime ago I met a war widow who became a living inspiration for me. Padma, who had lost her husband during the Kargil war, told me that she was fighting for her dues and rights against all odds, so that she could raise her son in the right manner. "I can't ruin my son's life by wallowing in my grief. He needs me more than ever and I will give him everything that my husband had wanted to provide him." I looked at her with pride and wished there were more Padmas in this world.

All sorrows, miseries and pain fade with time, no matter how great. No one can carry the same intensity of misery throughout life. Allow your grief to settle down and give your heart the time it needs to heal the wounds of the past. You will be surprised how soon that happens if we go about this in a positive manner.

No matter how grave the problems or how deep our loss, time is the greatest healer of all.

◆◆◆

Discover God in Every Soul

Even the worst criminal has a beautiful soul. God gave us all a beautiful soul but we may have failed to keep it beautiful. Those who sin are not evil; their souls still harbour the purity with which they were born. It is just that they have lost their way in life and need to be brought back to the right path. The soul is indestructible, the *Bhagavad Gita* teaches us. It remains untouched by the impurities that surround us and retains the purity with which the Almighty created it.

God resides in each of us. Sometimes, during our low phases, we lose touch with God. We become depressed and feel there is no justice in the world. We deny ourselves

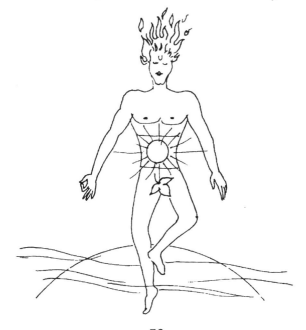

the luxury of being religious. Religion has a way of helping us overcome all adversities. It brings hope and light where there is darkness. It is a mechanism of coping gifted to each of us. We just have to reach out and embrace religion to be touched by hope.

Religion does not necessarily imply meaningless rituals. It means the ability to seek God through a direct approach from the spirit. It is faith in the ultimate deliverance that matters. If you have faith that things will work for you and that there is a superior being keeping watch over you, you will remain optimistic.

What is religion? It is a system of behaviour and application of truth by which man can remove threefold suffering: of body, mind and soul. There are two kinds of people in the world. The first are people who become cynical and pessimistic when things don't go their way. The second are those who rush to temples and God when things look bleak. They pray and beg the Almighty to set things right. Why don't the latter do it on a regular basis? Why does it take adversities and problems to make them seek God?

A few minutes of silence each day, trying to remember God, works wonders. This will impart peace of mind and a calm outlook that will help us cope with life's daily irritants and adversities. Beginning each day with hymns or spiritual music awakens the mind in a healthy, peaceful manner and equips the person to deal with the day in a positive way.

For peace and tranquillity, reach out and discover God within you.

◆◆◆

Ethics and Morality

Uneasy sleeps the mind that harbours unhealthy and sinful thoughts. Living with truth is so much easier. If we cheat people during the day, how can we sleep well at night? Moral convictions are magical mantras that keep us from straying. Religion is nothing but the path of truth. Unfortunately, we mistake rituals and beliefs to be true religion. We conduct pujas, chant mantras and perform rituals, which mean nothing if we perform them and then carry on with our dirty business, thereafter.

Hindus believe in *karma*. What is *karma*? It is the acts that you commit and the consequences thereof. Good *karma* brings good results and bad *karma* brings bad results. Every true philosophy teaches that whatever we sow in this world today is what we will reap someday. You can't plant a neem tree and expect apples! When you plant the seeds of wrong action, those seeds will bear bitter fruit. Lord Buddha has also promoted this theory in his teachings about the Path of Right Action.

We all have a body and a soul. We care so much for the body, cleaning it scrupulously, adorning it with ornaments and clothes, and spending much time pampering it. But do we pay a second thought to our soul? Do we bother to adorn it with beautiful thoughts, beautify it with good deeds or pamper it with right actions? Of course, we don't! If we did for our souls even a tenth of what we do for the body, we would be immensely happy.

It is never too late, though. Through positive thoughts, let us remove the dirt that surrounds our beautiful soul.

Pamper your soul with right thoughts, good deeds and compassionate love for all beings. ◆◆◆

Carpé Diem

The expression *Carpé Diem* is Latin for *Seize the day*. It is such a beautiful thought that I have made it my motto. Each day of our life is an important one. If are able to seize each day and make the most of it, we could get started on the path to happiness. Often we laze, loll and suspend things for another day. This causes us a lot of problems as we keep getting behind schedule. Living each moment in a manner that demands the utmost from it is a simple way of remaining cheerful. If we decide to do our bit each day – be it work, enjoyment, charity, worship – would it not be excellent?

Each sunrise ushers in a new day, and each day is a gift from God, to be cherished and lived honestly. Each day is a fresh opportunity to begin life anew, to learn new skills, to cement and foster new relationships, to undo past mistakes and establish new friendships.

Just as the new dawn heralds a new beginning, we shouldn't forget to thank the Almighty for giving us another chance to make amends and begin afresh. Even if you have made mistakes in the past, you can undo most of them by opening up your mind to fresh ideas.

Everyone makes mistakes, whether at work, home or at play, but that shouldn't make us lose hope. We should be willing to learn from our mistakes. What is important is that we must be willing to start afresh. Each day of our life is more important than the one that has passed.

Don't let the day slip by without attaining at least one objective.

◆◆◆

Keep Life Simple

Half our problems will disappear if we can simplify our lives. If you look back and think, you will realise that your childhood was so carefree and uncomplicated. Why was it uncomplicated? It was so because you didn't have ambitions and ego problems. Half our problems arise due to ambitions and the other half due to ego problems.

If you examine relationships gone sour, you will realise that almost all of them soured because of ego. If even one of the affected parties had come forward boldly and thrown ego out of the window, things would not have gone bad. Similarly, most of our frustrations, unhappiness and miseries arise from ambitions. If we downsize our ambitions, many of our problems would vanish.

All seers, godmen and scriptures advocate simplicity of life and thought. Yet, we can barely live a simple life. In order to be happy, you have to give up certain things. Why not begin by giving up a simple thing each year? If you give up smoking this year, try giving up non-vegetarian food the next year and silks or jewellery the year after that. Step by step, you can make a difference in your life.

A simple life doesn't necessarily mean you have to live in a hut and wear khadi; it means giving up things that lead you towards unhappiness, even if indirectly. If you give up wearing silks and jewellery, for instance, you will bring down your cost of living, which in turn will reduce your needs. Reduced needs mean less ambition and less greed. It helps you get out of the rat race. Get the point?

Simplicity of thought and deed and a simple life can reduce stress levels magically. ◆◆◆

Time for Introspection

Be able to be alone. Lose not the advantage of solitude, and the society of thyself.

—Sir Thomas Browne

Solitude can be blissful. It can provide the much-needed time for introspection and self-assessment. One needs to pause for a while before racing ahead. It gives you the momentary pause to focus on your self-growth. You need to pause from time to time in order to look back and see the path you have travelled, to assess whether it is the right path or you need to alter your course. There is a difference between being alone and being by yourself to meditate and mull over serious matters.

Human beings need to walk on the path of self-discovery and realise their potentials and weaknesses. This journey into self-discovery is a refreshing experience. Most of us are so busy running the rat race that we never pause and ponder. When we do not even know our own self, how will we attain success in our pursuits? If you pause for a few moments and introspect, you will perceive the gems lying dormant within you. It is only when you discover them that you can polish and use these gems for your benefit.

Even if you have suffered a major relationship crisis, you need to pause and think. You need to analyse where things went wrong and what could have been done to prevent the situation. For all this you need time and you need to introspect. Maybe it is not too late to make amends.

Whether it is your career or your relationships, the two most important areas in a person's life, you will surely fare much better if you devote some time in solitude and introspection over various aspects of your life. The best part of the journey into self-discovery is the discovery of your hidden talents and learning how to tap them.

Time spent on introspection sometimes changes your entire outlook towards life and sets you in a new direction altogether.

We have all read the story about the Mauryan emperor, Ashoka, who ruled India from 273–232 BC. Ashoka was a great emperor who managed to unite large, fragmented parts of India, and his empire consisted of what is today India, Pakistan and Afghanistan. After he fought the Battle of Kalinga, he spent time with himself and did some soul searching. The exercise changed the course of his life. The horrors of war sickened him and he realised the futility of bloodshed and violence.

He then renounced his desires and turned to Buddhism, spending the rest of his life in the spread of Buddhism. Ashoka made Buddhism the State religion. Religion gave him vision, wisdom and courage. His administration improved and people prospered.

Introspection leads to many benefits and helps in self-judgement. Setting aside time for introspection can set you on the path to happiness.

◆◆◆

Know Your Strengths

There is nothing lost by discarding your faults.

—Sophia Bedford-Pierce

In order to love ourselves we need to have high self-esteem and to develop that kind of self-esteem we must know our strengths and weaknesses. If you identify your weaknesses, you can work on them and turn them into positive traits. Similarly, if you know your strengths you can put them to work in a way that will maximise their power and potential.

My friend Madhu had severe doubts about her ability to sing. She rated herself as a bathroom singer, nothing more. During a camp where everyone had to sing before the campfire, Madhu refused to sing. She finally gave in to peer pressure and sang. Everyone was amazed at how well she sang. Even Madhu had not realised her true potential. She entered music contests thereafter and won many prizes.

What brought about the transformation? Madhu was unaware of her latent talents and lacked self-confidence but when she was forced to sing in public during the campfire, she realised her own strength, began working on it and achieved amazing results.

Conversely, Anil prided himself on being a great singer but never made it to the final rounds of any contest. After a while, this led to a fall in his self-esteem. Then he met a music teacher and took some classes. Together they identified Anil's weakness of not being able to control his breath. Once the weakness was identified, it was a matter of days before they achieved the desired results.

My father had wanted me to be an architect. I studied mechanical drawing for a few years till I realised that I was not really interested in it. I did my graduation in science since my mother wanted me to be a doctor. But I couldn't get into medical college. I spent half my life in the wrong field till I discovered my talent for writing. I left a lucrative job as an HR professional and took up writing. I began from scratch and continued working hard to hone my talent. The rest is for readers to gauge. But I know one thing – discovering my writing capabilities and using these skills has made me a very happy and content person. I couldn't have found the same joy as an architect or doctor.

Everybody needs to spend time discovering their aptitude and then honing it. If you love yourself, you must undertake the exercise because discovering a talent will provide an immense boost to your self-confidence and work wonders in your life. It could change the entire course of events. When you work in a field of your interest, it is much more enjoyable and affords greater joy.

Make an inventory of your strengths and weaknesses and then work on them to attain your goals in life.

◆◆◆

Keep Expectations Low

If you accept the expectations of others, especially negative ones, then you never will change the outcome.

—Michael Jordan

Expectations are perhaps the main cause of all our frustrations. We expect certain benefits from our careers, relatives, friends, colleagues and children. These are either monetary or intangible in nature. When our expectations are not met, we sulk and brood in unhappiness.

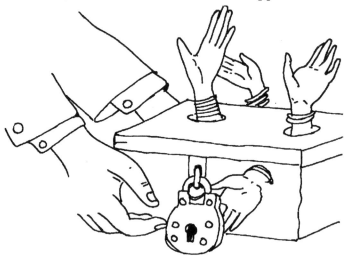

Throughout our lives, we base much of our happiness on expectations. When we are children, we expect our parents to fulfil most of our needs and desires. When we grow up, we expect our friends to live up to our expectations. After marriage, we have certain expectations from our spouse. When we begin working we have a long list of expectations from our boss, colleagues and the job. Again, when we have children, we expect them to meet certain standards academically and feel let down when they are unable to perform up to the standards set by us. When we are old, we expect our children to look after us. Thus the cycle of expectations goes on endlessly throughout our lives.

For a minute, just imagine not having expectations from anyone! Would life not be much easier and happier? If we don't expect children to perform according to our standards but simply as per their abilities, both parents and children would be satisfied and content. Similarly, if we don't expect the spouse to live up to our expectations, the number of broken marriages would come down drastically. If we didn't expect too much from our careers but worked sincerely, the job would give us much more happiness. In the *Bhagavad Gita*, Lord Krishna advises us not to think about the outcome but to perform our tasks sincerely. The results will follow.

If we work on our relationships, career and duties without worrying about the benefits, we would be very successful in our endeavour. Besides, we would never feel frustrated or let down because our expectations were not met.

Keep your expectations low but the responsibilities high.

Don't Short Sell Yourself

The minute you settle for less than you deserve, you get even less than you settled for.

—Maureen Dowd in *New York Times*

We often deserve what we get. I have come across an amazing number of people who don't realise their worth. Whenever I'm introduced to a homemaker, she invariably begins with: "Oh, I do not do anything, I am just a housewife." Does that mean household chores are worthless and not important enough to be termed a job? I promptly tell them they are doing the most important job in the world and without them the family would collapse.

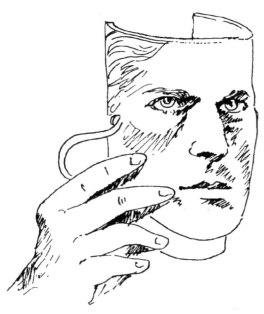

During my early years as a homemaker, I lacked confidence in my home-making skills; especially my cooking. Whenever we had guests, I always apologised for not being a good cook.

One day, an elderly relative came for dinner and as usual I apologised for my cooking. "Never say you can't cook. Don't ever make the mistake of saying that because people will never value your effort. Every housewife is good at her job in some way or the other. Don't undersell your skills by making foolish statements," he admonished me.

After the meal, he complimented me heartily: "I thought you said you couldn't cook! This is one of the best meals I've ever had."

That taught me two things – have confidence in your work and never short sell yourself. If you do, you will never receive due acknowledgement for your efforts. No matter how you picture yourself, you cannot feel worthwhile if you settle for less than you deserve. When it comes to self-esteem, how you treat yourself is just as important as how others treat you.

Know your capabilities and feel confident about them.

◆◆◆

Don't Seek Perfection

Do you believe there is perfection in this world? Don't even bother to answer this question! There is nothing in the world that is perfect and never will be. Yet, we all chase the mirage of perfection relentlessly throughout our lives. And what do we achieve? Frustration, unhappiness, misery and tension! So, is it really worth the effort?

I was a perfectionist for almost 30 years of my life. I began early in my childhood, being fastidious about everything, striving for perfection. I never liked anything less than perfect, yet I couldn't find the standards of perfection I desired, neither in myself nor in others. One sentence that I always added to all my statements was: 'I am particular about...' I was particular about almost everything. Whether it was my house, my career, my relationships or my possessions, I was particular about everything and nothing less would please me.

As a result I was a highly-strung person, always looking for faults to rectify. I was diagnosed as a Type A personality, which meant high stress and a highly volatile atmosphere at home. I couldn't sleep well and found myself grinding my teeth over trivial matters. If the children messed up the bed I would scream, if my husband left the toothpaste without its cap on the bathroom shelf, I threw a fit. I shouted at the maid because she didn't sweep the floor properly, I ranted at the gardener because I found weeds in the garden. I blew my top at work because someone had not met the deadline. I fought at the bank because the cashier was lethargic and slow. I had altercations at the supermarket because they over-billed me. Life was an endless struggle and my blood pressure shot up each time I interacted with someone.

Things began to go out of control and I sought my doctor's help. It was on his recommendation that I did a course in Vipassana meditation and found myself gaining some control over my emotions. I also realised that my pursuit of perfection was getting me more trouble than I could handle.

I learnt the hard way that seeking perfection is pointless.

If one stops trying to change things or find perfection in everyone and everything around him, he will definitely be in a much happier frame of mind. That does not mean anything goes – it just implies that things beyond your control should not bother you. Do your best but don't expect others to be perfect. We live in a world full of imperfections and striving for perfection can only cause a lot of unhappiness.

Perfection is a Utopia that exists only in the minds of perfectionists.

◆◆◆

Sleep Like a Baby

Sleep is the best cure for waking troubles.

—Cervantes

Few things are more important than a good night's sleep. After a good sleep you are much more alert. Lack of sleep makes a person slower and duller. During sleep, the body is busy repairing itself. Growth hormones pour into the body and stimulate various tissues and organs to repair themselves and grow. This is one reason why growing children need more sleep than adults. Even the brain is repairing itself during sleep and while this happens, blood supply to the brain increases and a person experiences a more wakeful period of dreaming sleep. Good sleep is essential for this process of bodily renewal, and if a person does not catch up on lost sleep, he loses the ability to concentrate and deal with the simplest of problems.

Most of us have inadequate or restless sleep when under stress. We struggle to sleep throughout the night and wake up feeling more tense and tired in the morning. Sleep is an essential part of our life. It rejuvenates and refreshes us. Sleep-deprived people often suffer various ailments because they don't get enough rest. Our bodies as well as minds need to relax and restore their energies. Complete relaxation only comes from deep and trouble-free slumber. Tense minds are often too active to benefit from sleep.

On many occasions you may have tossed from side to side throughout the night, because your mind was anxious about some matter. The following morning, you would have woken up feeling depressed and the day would have gone very badly. This happens because your body and mind were unable to refresh themselves with a good night's rest. So what is the remedy? Well, bear these pointers in mind to have a peaceful night's sleep:

- Maintain a regular sleep-wake pattern. Go to bed and wake up at the same time each day. Also, do not awaken too late, because the early morning sunlight is best at resetting your biological clock.

- Don't exercise strenuously within two to three hours of retiring. Exercising early in the day helps you sleep, but exercising too close to bedtime keeps you awake.

- Don't eat a large meal within one to two hours of going to bed. Major digestive efforts can keep you awake.

- Have a light snack before bed. A small amount of food before bed can help you sleep.

- Adopt bedtime rituals. Read for a while. Change into your nightdress. Brush your teeth. Lock the doors. Turn out the lights. Rituals help ease you into sleep.

- Regulate the air-conditioner. Cool temperatures help induce sleep.

- Don't nap during the day. Napping can interfere with night sleep.

- Limit caffeine consumption. Drink less regular coffee. Caffeine is also found in tea, colas, cocoa, chocolate, and many over-the-counter drugs (read labels and ask the chemist). Avoid caffeinated drinks eight hours before sleep.

- Avoid shift work. If at all possible, work days (9 to 5 or a schedule close to it). Working afternoons (4 to midnight) and nights (midnight to 8) disrupts sleep. The most sleep-disrupting schedule is rotating shift work: periods of day, afternoon, and night work.

- Hot milk with chocolate or a warm shower helps unwind the body. Listening to soothing music also calms our minds and induces sleep.

Sleep is essential for well-being and happiness.

◆◆◆

Know Your Priorities

Often I come across people who are trying to do too many things at the same time. And what is the end result? Well, they are neither able to complete all that they intended to do nor can they achieve any quality in their work. At the end of the day they are a harassed and unhappy lot. To add to their woes, they can't sleep well at night because they feel that they have not been able to achieve all that they set out to do.

If you are such a person, here is a piece of advice – don't take on too much work. The solution is simple – prioritise. We have just two hands, two feet and one brain, so how can we perform superhuman feats? When we try to juggle two or three things together, we are unable to give our best to any of them. This is exactly what quality time is all about. When you give quality time to anything, it simply means being 100% with the task at hand. There should be no distractions and no stress.

The best thing would be to make a list of the tasks for the day and put priority numbers on them. If you have to handle six tasks, simply assign priority values to them and then go about performing those tasks. That way, you will neither be hassled nor will your work suffer.

Prioritising is not just about task performance – it is also about other matters of life. For instance, a woman should know whether her family is a priority or her career. Similarly, a man must know whether money is his priority or happiness. You can't have everything in life and one has to sacrifice something in order to gain another thing.

When you know that your home and family come first, you can always opt for careers that help you maintain both, with equal efficiency. I have come across many women who do not want to give up their jobs, even if they could, but lament the lack of time they have for their children. One has to choose at some stage in life.

Ashok is unable to decide whether his business is more important than his wife and children. He is so busy with his factory that he returns home at a very late hour and has no time for interaction with his family. As a result, the children have drifted away from him and his wife has also found other means of solace. When Ashok turned 60, his children had gone their own way and he found himself totally isolated because even his wife did not have anything to communicate and the distance between them was unbreachable. At the fag end of his life, Ashok realised he had been chasing the wrong priorities.

On the other hand, Tarun has always maintained that his family comes first. No matter what his compulsions, he puts his wife and children first on the priority list. As a result, he is a happy, content man although he may not have reached the top of his career. But he had always maintained that career was his second priority.

Choose what you value more in life and follow that value. Not knowing priorities can land a person in a very unhappy situation.

Life is all about knowing one's priorities and goals for happiness.

◆◆◆

Manage Time Efficiently

I recommend you take care of the minutes, for the hours will take care of themselves

—Lord Chesterfield

Ask anyone about how he is doing and he is likely to complain that he doesn't have the time. Ask the children whether they have practised a game or music or finished their homework and they will complain they didn't have the time. Adult or child, one thing in common is that no one has the time to do all that they want to. Whether it is at work or at home, one needs to pack in a lot of activity within 24 hours of the day.

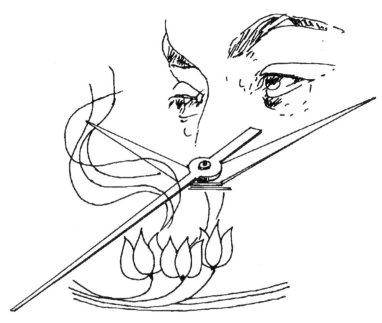

Time management has become the most important thing in our lives. We have been reduced to living by the clock and our lives are becoming more and more mechanical. But time and tide wait for no one. If we can't complete something in time, we won't keep pace with the times. Time management is essentially about sorting out the important and unimportant tasks and assigning priorities to those that need to be done during the day. Once a person learns to do that there is no dearth of time to perform whatever one sets out to. Time management is a set of related common-sense skills that help you use your time in the most effective and productive way possible.

Pad your schedule. Realise that nearly everything will take longer than you anticipate. By allotting yourself enough time to accomplish a task, you cut back on anxiety. In general, if meeting deadlines is a problem, always give yourself 20 per cent more time than you think you need to do the task.

A few guidelines:

- Determine what is important and what can be dropped.
- Use spare time in the most effective manner possible.
- Increase the time allotted for each work.
- Control distractions that waste time and break the flow.
- Increase effectiveness and reduce stress.

Time is the most valuable asset. It can't be bought nor retrieved once it is lost. Make the most of this priceless element.

◆◆◆

Energy Highs and Lows

There are two important things that determine the quantity and quality of our work: the time spent on it and the quantum of energy expended on it. If we are low on either element, we will fail to do justice to the work.

More and more people complain about the lack of energy in their everyday lives. Young people who should be at their peak complain about feeling exhausted by evening. Time was when people walked for hours and did much more manual labour than we do today, yet remained energetic and happy at the end of the day, slept well and woke up refreshed. What has caused the change?

Our lifestyle! Stress, environmental pollution, wrong food habits and other things have taken their toll on our energy levels. We can't control pollution at individual levels but we can certainly alter our food habits and stress levels.

You may find that your energy levels throughout the day are driven by your eating patterns. Having a good breakfast with plenty of carbohydrates will keep your brain supplied with sugars for the early part of the day. These sugars fade sharply by mid-morning as your body reacts to high levels of sugar by burning it faster and then the supplies run down. Some people find a mid-morning snack useful to avoid this. Other people recommend having protein (e.g., an egg) for breakfast. This delays the energy dip.

Conversely, eating a large lunch diverts blood from your brain towards digestion – you have probably felt sleepy after a heavy meal. This will be worse if you drink alcohol at lunch because it is a sedative.

You may also find that energy levels are dependent on whether you take rest or not. If you work through the day with no breaks, you may fade badly in end-afternoon. Often, a lunch break allows you to start the afternoon refreshed for quality work. With intelligent eating and adequate breaks you can extend the amount of quality time available to you in a day quite significantly.

Try experimenting with different eating and rest patterns to see which ones suit the way you work. It is worth trying each approach for a few days before deciding on what suits you.

Pep up your life with the right combination of nutrition and work out the right rest periods, which can invigorate you and make you feel sprightly right through the day.

Recharging your cells in the right manner can make you feel bright and peppy throughout the day.

◆◆◆

Strength and Courage

What I want is muscles of iron and nerves of steel, inside which dwells a mind of the same material as that of which the thunderbolt is made.

—Swami Vivekananda

Is mental strength more important than the physical one? Somebody once asked me this question and I answered: "Yes! It is more important to have a strong mind than to possess a powerful body because a strong body without a strong mind is of no use. Yet, a strong mind with a weak body can still function quite remarkably."

Remember the story of David and Goliath? Wasn't Goliath much bigger and physically stronger than David?

Yet, David could slay the giant without any problems because he was mentally strong. The mind is all-powerful and potent. Used well, it shows us the direction for the right path.

This mental strength and courage is most required when we face adversities. Those strong in the mind can overcome any adversity and emerge cheerfully from the experience, much stronger than before. You may build muscles by pumping iron but if your mind is weak of what use are muscles? So, develop mental strength.

"Strength is life, weakness is death; strength is felicity, life eternal, immortal! Weakness is constant strain and misery. Weakness is death. Let positive, strong, helpful thoughts enter into your brains from very childhood," exhorted Swami Vivekananda. "Weakness is the one cause of suffering. We become miserable because we are weak."

Vivekananda was not referring to weakness of the body but to weakness of the soul. When we have a mind that is strong as steel, we automatically have the will power and strength to emerge from our sorrows and lead a happy life.

Mental strength is more important than physical strength.

◆◆◆

Loneliness Can be Depressing

Apart from stress, one of the ills of modern living is loneliness. The curse of loneliness is extremely depressing for most people. With our busy lives, we have built steel walls around ourselves, which keep others away. In the past, there was no television, VCD and the Internet. So people spent time communicating with each other and enjoyed pastimes that promoted togetherness. So, the community factor was very strong and people rushed to help anyone in need without waiting to be asked to do so. Today, most of us are too busy to visit people or keep in touch. And the little time we have is spent before the television.

All these factors have left people feeling isolated and lonely. Loneliness in turn leads to depression, pessimism and cynicism. This is especially true for people who live in metropolitan cities where apartments are big barriers

to community living. One has to just enter an old age home to realise the depth of loneliness suffered by the neglected and the aged. The misery of isolation is writ large on their hapless faces.

Loneliness is greatest in countries that value independence compared to those societies where community living is the norm. Loneliness causes great emotional pain that makes it difficult to make friends and meet new people. Greater the loneliness, the harder it is to remedy. Therefore, the first step to alleviate loneliness lies in addressing the emotional pain and finding a way to be by oneself without feeling lonely and isolated.

When she was 23, my friend Sarita's daughter, Alisha, walked out of home to live on her own. Alisha had a good job, many friends and hobbies. But after she returned from work and entered her flat, she felt a sense of heavy loneliness because her friends were not there for company. After a while she begged her parents to take her back because she could not tolerate the loneliness any longer. Although she had sought independence and a less restrictive life, she couldn't combat the loneliness that living alone entailed.

How does one deal with loneliness? By promoting human contact and realising that life is not about living for oneself but for living with others.

It is not essential that living with a family can cure loneliness; what one needs are healthy relationships. If someone lives in a large house with many family members, but is ensconced in his room and does not interact with others, he would still feel the pain of loneliness. Regular communication and interaction with others keeps loneliness at bay.

Loneliness can only be tackled through proper interactions and relationships.

◆◆◆

Investing in Others

There is no investment as fruitful as one in relationships. This requires spending time with people in a meaningful manner. It means being available for friends and relatives when they need you and being emotionally honest with them. If loneliness has taught me one thing, it's the value of an honest friend. Even in a relationship, one can feel lonely. This happens when one is habituated and desensitised to the presence of the other person and takes the other for granted.

Most relationships these days are based on greed and self-interest. The moment you are introduced to someone, the person begins calculating how much of an asset you will prove to be, whether it is worth investing time on you and if you will return favours or not. It is these calculations that come in the way of emotional honesty, which implies being a part of a relationship without any expectations or ulterior motives, simply because you like a person or enjoy being with him. A person who interacts with others selflessly never suffers loneliness.

Loneliness is hard to heal. It requires more than just casual social contact. You need to bond honestly with others on a one-to-one basis. If loneliness is to be healed, it needs more investment of time. It requires constant interaction with others and loads of patience and endurance until our efforts culminate in a sincere relationship.

Friendship is one of the best investments we can make.

◆◆◆

Giving Brings Joy

You give but little when you give of your possessions. It is when you give of yourself that you truly give.

—Kahlil Gibran in *The Prophet*

When it comes to giving, we are all miserly and petty. We want something all the time but never talk of giving.

Some time ago I visited an orphanage to give a few clothes away. I was directed to an anterior room where I could leave my package. When I entered the room, I was surprised. Bundles of clothes, piled up high, occupied one corner of the room while books, games, fruits etc, were piled in the other corners. I realised my clothes were not needed – the orphanage had enough already.

When I asked the manager why the room was filled with so many things and whether they needed any more clothes, he replied: "Madam, there are many rich people in this city and most of them bring something or the other that they don't need. We do not need any more clothes or books. What we need is people's time. We want people to come and talk to these orphans and spend time with them. They need company and reassurance more than they need new clothes."

Then realisation struck me. We all give material things and think that we are doing charity but none of us wants to invest time. *We are most stingy with our time and that is what is most needed.*

Sometimes we grow so accustomed to wants and needs that we forget we have anything to give. Others may need us more than we need them, even though habit leads us to expect the opposite. If each of us decides to devote even one hour in a week towards alleviating someone's misery, we could wipe out most of the unhappiness and misery around us. The best part of the giving is that we do ourselves a favour when we give something to others because we are most benefited by the act. God returns hundredfold what we give others. And the joy that giving brings is equalled by nothing on earth.

Giving is a joyful experience that benefits the giver more than the receiver.

◆◆◆

Nurture Your Marriage

Marriage is something you have to give your whole mind to.
—Henrik Ibsen

Research indicates that happily married people live much longer than single ones and have a healthy constitution – mental, emotional and physical. Marriage is a relationship that can bring a lifetime of support and love.

Most of us do not invest enough time and effort to nurture our marriage, disregarding the fact that this is the only relationship that may last lifelong. A survey on the factors for happiness placed happy marriages on top of the list. Sadly, more and more marriages are breaking up these days because no one is interested in putting the extra effort required to maintain marital harmony.

It is quite simple really. Man or woman, humans are social beings. We marry, have children and rejoice in family bonds. A happy family can bring much contentment to people but happy families can only emerge from happy marriages. If the husband and wife are unhappy together, can they create a happy atmosphere at home?

The foundation of a society is the family and the pillar of a happy family is a stable and happy marriage. So it makes much sense to invest time and effort in creating marital bliss if one wants to live happily ever after.

Happy marriages bring about happiness in life.

◆◆◆

Be More Social

Man is a social animal.

—Seneca

Man has been a social animal right from the beginning of civilisation. Even caveman moved in a group and belonged to a clan. The sense of belonging to a particular group of people brought emotional and physical security to man. Thereafter, as we progressed, we founded new codes and modes of socially acceptable behaviour that helped humans restrain themselves and live in a moral orbit drawn by society.

There are many advantages in being a part of society. No one can live his entire life in seclusion. Even those who seem socially disenchanted live within the ambit of society in many ways. Those who live a full life, actively interacting with people, have a much happier life than those living in isolation. Being useful to society and leading an active social life is a saving grace for those who have suffered some kind of tragedy. The social interaction helps in overcoming lean periods.

When young, we gloat over the fact that we don't need anyone and are happiest if left alone to do our own thing. Anyone who is healthy, with a good job and a reasonably comfortable lifestyle, feels he can buck the norms of society. But as one ages, the need to belong begins to haunt a person. He strives for a socially acceptable lifestyle. When he marries and has children, the need to fit into society becomes more imperative. Thereafter, when he grows old, the need is greater and he finds himself becoming socially active and seeking ways and means to do something useful for society.

Belonging brings a sense of joy and fulfilment in our lives. Recognition, acceptance and usefulness also bring happiness. When appreciated for our contribution to a cause, we feel a sense of achievement and contentment. Active social life ensures many friends and well-wishers who rally around us in times of crisis. When sick, we feel the need for friends and relatives more than ever. Similarly, when we need some help, friends do their bit.

The greatest sense of belonging comes when we contribute our mite for the unprivileged. This makes our lives more meaningful and happy. Sharing our joys and material things again leads to a sense of contentment.

Finally, discover happiness in relationships with friends and family. Make your interactions more meaningful. Let people know how much you care for them. Spend time together. Work to make your relationships more close-knit. Having someone to talk to, when it seems the rest of the world is against you, can be a great comfort and promote happiness. Spend more time with people who make you feel good about yourself and inspire you.

Isolation brings depression and pessimism while social interactions bring joy and happiness.

◆◆◆

Children Ensure Happiness

There is no friendship, no love, like that of the parent for the child.

—Henry Ward Beecher

We may rant and rave when our children trouble us but the fact is that they bring more joy to our hearts than we can imagine. Children make our life much brighter. Ask a couple who are childless and they will tell you how empty and shallow their lives are.

The mischievous laughter and carefree prattle of children give us the greatest pleasure. Can you forget the first smile of your baby, the first words, his first step in this world, his first day at school, the first song he sang and the first time he rode a bicycle? No one can. These are unforgettable landmarks in our lives. No matter how much we achieve in our career, the achievements of our children remain the greatest joy. We can suffer immense pain but a little pain suffered by the child fills us with anguish.

Life is a cycle. Our parents did for us what we are now doing for our children. A well-brought up child is the ultimate achievement of a human being. When we raise socially well-adjusted and morally upright children, we do great service to humanity. Therefore, investing time and energy in your children ensures far more happiness than anything else.

A child is a joy forever.

◆◆◆

Care for Your Parents

Next to God, thy parents.

—William Penn

Indian culture has taken pride in caring and obeying parents. Sadly, our youth are now going the western way, with more and more elderly people being neglected by their children. Many children feel that doling out some money for their parents' maintenance is enough to rid them of guilt. But a person who neglects his parents will be hounded by guilt forever and never live in peace and happiness.

We must also remember one thing. Our children are watching how we deal with our parents and this is the way they will treat us when we grow old! Then, we will be in no position to complain about our children neglecting us. We reap what we sow. If we show concern, love and respect for our parents, we could expect the same from our children. But if we treat our parents shabbily, we can expect the same from our children.

It is essential to reciprocate the love our parents gave us. They sacrificed their comforts for ours, they stayed awake through the nights so that we could sleep, and they lived a life of denial so that we could fulfil our wants. In return, if we cannot give them a little happiness during their twilight years, it will be the biggest sin we commit. A man who takes care of his parents and keeps them in comfort will live a happy life because of his parents' blessings.

Looking after our parents will earn us blessings that will ensure joy and happiness in our lives.

◆◆◆

Develop Creative Hobbies

When I was in the fifth standard, my teacher always cited a famous adage: *A man without hobbies is like a rudderless ship.* So many of us rush through our lives without developing any creative hobby simply because we have no time. We lead a clockwork life, rushing from one task to the other, without pausing for a moment to think what will happen when we retire. And do we ever pause to think whether we do anything that gives us real joy.

Hobbies fill up that gap in our life where joy and contentment lie hidden. When we do something that gives us pleasure, our stress levels are in control and the emotional fulfilment derived from such activities results in tremendous happiness. For instance, a person who loves painting but does not find time to do so will definitely feel a sense of dissatisfaction at some level. But if he sets aside a couple of hours every weekend to enjoy his hobby, would it not bring a sense of immense satisfaction and joy to him?

Any creative activity that we undertake uplifts our soul. Classical music, painting, playing an instrument – these are all spiritual activities that bring a lot of peace to the mind. When you sing or write you are lost in the world of art and creativity, away from humdrum activities and the stress of living in today's frenetic world.

Finally, when we retire from active life and have nothing to do, we feel miserable. But setting aside a few hours for creative activities can help us build a reservoir of interests that will stand by us when we have time on hand.

A hobby can keep us positively occupied.

Religion and Prayer

Religion is not in doctrines, in dogmas, nor in intellectual argumentation; it is being and becoming; it is realisation.

—Swami Vivekananda

Most of us confuse religion with rituals. We perform puja, observe fasts and chant mantras without understanding anything about them. But that is not religion. Religion is how we uplift our spirit and soul. It is about how we behave and lead our lives.

I am a great admirer of Swami Vivekananda. He was one of the greatest sons of India. If only there were a few more of his ilk, our country would lead the world. Swamiji said: "Can religion really accomplish anything? It can. It brings to man eternal life. It has made man what he is, and will make of this human animal a God. This is what religion can do. Take religion from human society and what will remain? Nothing but a forest of brutes."

Why is religion so powerful? Why do we rush to pray whenever things are not going the right way? Because religion can bring relief and solace. Everyone cannot become an enlightened person but we can lead a righteous life, which is the best religion one can follow. According to Thomas Fuller: "A good life is the only religion."

Religion and prayers are the biggest stress busters and most doctors recommend that one spend a few minutes every day in prayer. When you pray, you find hope and light. It helps you get over the lows in life. It brings peace and joy to the soul. What more reason does one need to pray and become religious?

At one point in my life I was an atheist and took pride in saying that there was no God. I had suffered tremendous setbacks and become cynical. Then the good times rolled in and I felt scared that I would lose all this once more. It was during this time that I began praying and thanking God for giving me the joyous years. Man is selfish by nature. He does not remember God or thank Him for anything till he suffers. If he prays regularly, would he not find more happiness and contentment, besides finding the strength to cope with setbacks?

What are the most effective prayers? Our thoughts, our words and our actions are our prayers. The most powerful prayer is the one in which we thank God for everything that he has given us and express our gratitude. It comes straight from the heart and is infinite in nature.

It is also said that a family that prays together, stays together. So make it a family event to pray together every day. Set aside a certain time of the day, in the morning or evening, when all family members are present and just say a small thanksgiving prayer and see the difference it makes in the lives of everyone.

Prayers give us the strength and equanimity to withstand and traverse the dips in life.

◆◆◆

Lead a Stress-free Life

Adversity is the diamond dust heaven polishes its jewels with.

—Leighton

Anubhav had everything going for him. He was young, strong, and handsome, with a fantastic career and a beautiful wife. His friends envied him and thought that he was leading a charmed life. What they didn't know was that his profession was a high stress one. Three years later, at the age of 36 when Anubhav suffered his first heart attack, everyone was surprised – except his doctor. The kind of stress that had invaded the young man's life produced a host of ill effects. Then, nothing could come to the rescue.

Stress is the number one killer in current times. Most of our health problems are because of high stress levels. Stress and worry cause physical and emotional problems that damage both your health and performance. Worse, stress grows! Excessive worry is a major element in the vicious cycle of tension: the physical sensations of stress – tense muscles, headaches, insomnia and so forth – lead to catastrophic stress-building thoughts, which in turn aggravate unpleasant physical feelings.

Stress management skills are important for healthy living. Why? Over-zealous stress hormones negatively impact the heart, blood vessels and blood pressure. Specifically, hormone activity during stress will cause the heart to beat faster, the blood vessels to constrict (narrow) and the force of blood to increase. This combination spells trouble, especially for those who already have a vulnerable heart. It is also true that for many people undue or prolonged stress leads to unhealthy behaviour patterns like overeating, excessive alcohol, more cigarette smoking and even withdrawal from social and physical activities.

Managing stress well does not mean avoiding it altogether. This would be nearly impossible. Life presents us with challenges and stress is a natural response. Without some stress, there would hardly be any motivation to act. But if stress is easily and frequently aroused or if it lasts for an extended period, health begins to suffer. In addition to cardiovascular health, the immune system is also compromised by stress increasing our vulnerability to infection, immune disorders and even cancer.

Stress can be controlled through:

- Positive thinking skills.
- Spending regular time in deep relaxation.
- Expressing emotions and letting out steam.
- Humour and laughter.
- Keeping a pet.
- Cultivating hobbies.
- Music.

Be aware of stress in your life and your body's reaction to it. Awareness and proactive stress management will help you meet the challenges of life with less harmful effects on your heart and body. Besides, you will also enjoy the good feelings that emerge from stress management.

Stress control is the first step towards a peaceful and harmonious life.

Happiness is Within You

A poor temple priest owned two buckets. Every morning, the priest would fill the buckets and walk the distance from his hut to the temple, and perform his rituals. One of the buckets had several holes in it and most of the water would drain out before the priest reached the temple. The other bucket was in good condition and proud that it carried its water all the way to the temple. One day the good bucket jeered at the leaking bucket: "You are useless, my friend. All the water that should reach the temple just leaks out of you. What is the use of such a bucket? And are you happy with your performance?"

The leaking bucket smiled: "I have my uses. Look at the flowers that line the path to the temple. Since the priest carries me in his right hand, only the right side of the path is lined with flowers. The water that leaks out of me nurtures them. Look at the left side; it is all barren and dry because you don't spare a drop for the parched earth. If the water did not leak out of me, the beautiful flowers would not exist and the priest would have no flowers to offer the gods in the temple. You have a purpose and I have my purpose – so where is the question of being worthless? I am happy because I know my worth."

All of us have a specific purpose in life. God has created all men and women to do something that the others can't. Once we absorb this truth, we can easily find happiness and contentment and achieve all that is within our power. Since happiness is within us, isn't it foolish to look for it elsewhere?

God created human beings as happy beings. We have created our own unhappiness.

◆◆◆

Develop Strong Self-esteem

No one can make you feel inferior without your consent.
—Eleanor Roosevelt

Learn to value yourself. No matter what you've done in the past that you are ashamed or embarrassed of, leave it in the past. Recognise your own self-worth. Most of us are unable to appreciate the gifts that God has given us and keep hankering for things that others possess. Once we realise the talents and skills that we possess, we will be able to harness our energies and increase our sense of self-worth. This would enable us to love ourselves.

Loving ourselves does not mean we become narcissists, but simply that we find a sense of contentment by liking the way we are. Most of us simply do not love the way we are – we want longer hair, better complexion, better facial features, taller stature etc. As a result, we live in a continuous state of dissatisfaction just because we are "different" and do not know how to appreciate ourselves. A person who suffers from dissatisfaction and low self-esteem can neither be happy nor achieve anything.

A few years ago, I noticed my self-esteem varied wildly depending on what aspect of myself I was thinking about at the time. Thinking about my accomplishments made me feel really good and strong. But thinking about shortcomings left me dejected. To overcome this, I worked on integrating these disparate views of myself to ensure a more balanced outlook. When I felt high, I reminded myself that I also have a few flaws. When low, I recalled my achievements. This balance gave my self-esteem more stability.

Low self-esteem for a prolonged period may cause emotional, mental and even physical problems. In the worst form, it can lead to anxiety, stress or depression. Self-doubt and a sudden lack of confidence can be normal – just a defensive reaction to a high-pressure situation. Even the most successful people have occasional self-doubts.

If you find yourself less competent or incapable of meeting the daily demands of life, you need to bring about a positive change in yourself. Once you regain your sense of worth, your stress level will fall and the symptoms of anxiety or depression will disappear. The following tips will help boost your ego and enhance well-being:

- Think positive about problems and remember what you have accomplished successfully in the past.
- Do not introduce too many simultaneous changes in your life. Introduce any change gradually and give yourself and others sufficient time to adjust to it.
- Set short-term goals.
- Accept only achievable targets.
- Judge yourself and your strong points properly.
- Avoid alcohol to boost self-esteem.
- Learn to see yourself as an achiever.
- Do not dwell on the past; it cannot be altered.
- A positive self-image and a healthy attitude indicate a good level of self-esteem. This increases your resistance to stress-related problems and improves work efficiency. Work on improving your self-image and abandon negative feelings about yourself.

Develop confidence in yourself. Happiness and low self-esteem cannot co-exist.

◆◆◆

Don't Dwell in the Past; Live in the Present

The stories that you tell about your past shape your future.

—Eric Ransdell

The Yin and Yang of life (the Chinese concepts of the male and female power) guarantee that there will be ups and downs in life. This is a very good thing; otherwise, the ups would not be fully appreciated. If one lives with the philosophy that life will, eventually, balance things out, it becomes easier to deal with the lows of life.

We tend to hold on to our memories and the ones that are dear to us are the ones that are painful. We brood and tend to them because we don't want to part with them. These unhappy memories interfere with our present state of mind and happiness. The painful memories that haunt us are usually experiences that were never resolved. Regret, resentment and grudges chain us to things we cannot change.

Peace with the past does not necessarily mean finding answers. It means accepting things that happened just the way they happened. Life is all about forgetting what happened in the past and moving on. Even if the past was very happy, don't allow it to become the measure for your future. Take each day as it comes and live it to the hilt. As Deepak Chopra says: *"The past is history and the future is a mystery. It is the present which is a gift from God."*

Don't allow past memories to chain you down and slow your movements towards a bright future.

◆◆◆

Learn to Say 'No'

I find it difficult to say 'no'. It is one of the things I kept trying to but failed to learn, until recently. Even now, I am not really good at this and my inability to say 'no' has landed me in trouble many times. When you can't say 'no' people take you for granted and heap you with all kinds of impractical demands.

A few years ago, I received a call from a friend in Delhi. She told me that a relative of hers was visiting Bangalore and would stay with us. I agreed although I was going through a hectic period and wasn't keeping too well. The maid had taken leave and my daughter's exams were on, the deadline from my publishers was already over and I was weak after a viral fever. But I couldn't say 'no'. What my friend had neglected to say was that a clutch of her relatives was coming!

There were seven of them and they expected to be waited on hand and foot. They had different food habits – a few were vegetarians while a couple of them were non-vegetarians. The expectations were lofty, too. We were expected to take them on sightseeing tours around the city and adjoining areas. Within two days of cooking, cleaning and coping with their heavy and unrealistic demands I had a relapse and was laid up in bed. The guests left after a week by which time I was totally drained. My daughter fared badly as she had not been able to study with the house full of people, I couldn't meet my deadline, because of which I lost out on a contract.

All this wouldn't have happened if I had been able to say 'no'. There are umpteen such examples in our lives. Most of us are unable to say the dreaded word 'no' only because we are led by our emotions. We don't want to hurt anyone or lose his or her affection. But sometimes you must learn to draw the line.

Stressed-out people often can't assert themselves. If we fail to make the boundaries clear, they will be violated time and again, leaving us feeling helpless and powerless. However, when we draw a clear line, everyone feels better. We regain the sense of power and others know where we stand. There are no illusions or lofty expectations. Everything works out well in the end because we know our limitations and understand each other better. There are no misunderstandings, either.

People who are shouldering too much responsibility suffer immense stress because they cannot say 'no', especially to their bosses. At work, instead of saying 'I will not be able to do this' or 'I need some help', they do it all by themselves. Then they have even more to do!

Give your boss a choice. Say 'I'd really love to take this on, but I can't do it without postponing something else. Which of these things would you like me to do first?' Most bosses take the hint. The same strategy works at home, with your spouse, children, relatives and friends.

If you have trouble saying 'no', start small. Tell your hubby to make his own sandwich. Or tell your daughter to find her way home on her own after music practice. Life will be much easier when people don't take you for granted or heap unfair demands on you. The notion that saying 'no' is bad is the first thing you need to drop.

Learning to say 'no' prevents much unhappiness and stress.

◆◆◆

Be Flexible

Better bend than break.

—Scottish proverb

If you can turn this proverb into a guiding principle, you will never be unhappy. Bending according to the breeze keeps the reed standing. If it were rigid, it would snap and break. Flexibility is a tool that is bound to make you more relaxed and comfortable. When you are not rigid about things, your mind accepts changes easily. This makes it easier to deal with difficult issues in life.

If I sincerely believe something is wrong, I try not to let anyone persuade me otherwise. I do not allow anyone to make me tolerate something I sincerely believe should never be tolerated. Otherwise, I lose my defences and my identity. I lose every belief that I have nurtured throughout life. But that does not mean I am not open to learning. An open mind must allow the winds of change to sweep through it. I will bend backwards to accommodate a thought that can enlighten me or change my world.

On the other hand, if someone truly changes my mind about something, I am not losing power by making that change. No one ever really wins or loses an argument when the changes are sincere. To be stubborn and rigid is dangerous. We stop learning and growing the moment we adopt a rigid stance and close our minds. Flexibility gives us more control to adapt to the world. No one knows everything or is absolutely right at all times.

Happiness is all about changing and adapting to the world. Whenever an older generation has refused to change its way of thinking to suit the present world, they have suffered. Times and attitudes are changing. If we don't mould ourselves to current ways, we can never grow. Flexibility is about learning new things while retaining the old useful ones. It is also about replacing outdated and impractical ideas with modern, practical ones.

Abraham Lincoln once said in his speech in 1865: *"Important principles may and must be flexible."*

Flexibility facilitates growth.

◆◆◆

63

Live for Today,
Love for Tomorrow

Deepak Chopra, the new age guru, once said that the past is gone, the future is unknown and the present is a gift that one must enjoy. If we brood over past fallacies or glories and spend time thinking about what could have been and what had been, we will lose out on what is presently happening. And a futuristic approach doesn't really ensure a happy present.

Most Indians are known to horde money anticipating a miserable future and denying themselves small enjoyments in the present. Appreciate the things that are happening right now, enjoy the blissful days watching your children grow, and savour the vigour of your healthy, young body. These things will not last forever, so enjoy them NOW.

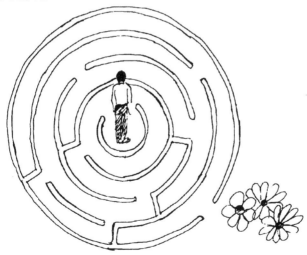

Over-planning for the future will ruin your present. One cannot live in the future. There is no guarantee you will live to see the future you are planning so meticulously. When we hoard and save, do we know that we will live till 60, 70 or 80 to use this wealth? Why spoil today for an uncertain tomorrow?

I have sometimes found myself unable to enjoy a moment of happiness because I was too worried I would fail to enjoy it! When this happens, I stop trying so hard, let go, and trust that happiness will come naturally. This approach works, although it is not always easy to implement. How much planning does it take to enjoy a moment? None!

While we must learn to enjoy each moment and live for the present, we also have to love for tomorrow. That means with each moment we invest in another person, we are sowing the seeds of love. The love we give our children, friends and relatives, or even the destitute, will return manifold tomorrow, when we need it most.

Today is all we are sure of; tomorrow is unseen, unknown and uncertain. So live in the present moment.
◆◆◆

Always Remember Someone with More Problems

In her book, *Island of Blood*, journalist Anita Pratap writes: "I have never experienced stress or fear or anxiety. When I am in the midst of a personal difficulty, I just remember the faces and the trauma of the Tamils and realise how trivial my problems are in comparison. Instead of railing against God for piling difficulties on my plate, I learnt to thank Him for giving me problems that were so ordinary, so mundane. It is this realisation – that life could be a million times worse – that has kept me happy since then."

She had written these lines after a visit to a refugee camp in Sri Lanka where Tamilians were housed after a racial riot. When one has witnessed the horrors that humans go through, little problems that hound us seem trivial. I am reminded of the physically challenged man's words: *"I cried about my limp till I met a man without limbs."*

Don't feel defeated by your little problems. Human beings can find immense strength and courage in the face of adversities and easily rise up to any challenge. All it takes is courage and endurance. People have gone through calamities and wars and yet surfaced with renewed hope and energy. There have been cases where people who lost everything emerged stronger from their experience. If they can find hope and happiness after major calamities, should we allow ourselves to be defeated by minor hassles?

When the going gets tough, the tough get going.

◆◆◆

Fight Anxiety

Did you know arthritis could be caused by broken marriages, worries, anxieties, financial problems and nursing past resentments? Anxiety is linked to fear and includes worry and panic. It arises in uncertain situations, when the prospect of danger lingers, and the result is an urge to flee or, if that is not possible, to fight. The body undergoes a transformation from a state of calm to a state of alarm. The heart and lungs work faster and the muscles tighten. When this response goes on for too long, the effects are painful and damaging.

Sigmund Freud, the founder of psychoanalysis, showed that anxiety is a fundamental emotion that influences our lives from earliest childhood. Anxiety occurs when you are concerned that circumstances are out of control. In some cases, anxiety and worry may generate a solution. But generally, it will have adverse effects.

There are five major unrealistic desires or beliefs that cause anxiety:

- The desire to always have the love and admiration of people important to you. This is unrealistic because you have no control over other people's minds. They may have their own views and agendas.
- The desire to be thoroughly competent at all times. This is unrealistic because you only achieve competence at a new level by making mistakes. Everybody has bad days and everybody makes mistakes.

- The belief that external factors cause all misfortune. Often, negative events can be caused by your negative attitudes. Similarly, your negative attitudes can cause you to view neutral events negatively.
- The desire that events should always turn out the way you want them to and people should do what you want is the cause of most anxieties. Others have their own agendas and do what they desire.
- The belief that past bad experiences will inevitably control what happens in the future. You can often improve or change things if you try hard enough or look at things in a different way.

Controlling these beliefs ensures you conquer anxiety.

An anxious mind is like a leaping flame. It destroys peace and happiness all around it.

Control Anger

Anger is momentary madness, so control your passion or it will control you.

—**Horace**, *Epistles*

There is no person on earth who has never felt anger at some point of time. Anger is a normal and even necessary emotion. But when anger is uncontrolled it can cause personal, professional and health problems.

Anger can be described as a strong feeling of displeasure. When angry, your heart rate and blood pressure increase. There are many things that may cause anger. When angry, you may rant and rave, work up your blood pressure, burst a blood vessel or simply simmer and fume. Whichever way you express the emotion, it is likely to cause more harm than good. Relationships may get ruined, jobs may be affected, people may be harmed and many things may go wrong if you cannot control your anger.

Can anger be controlled? Of course, it can!

Tips on Anger Management

You can't get rid of all your anger. Since anger is a normal emotion, there will always be circumstances that cause anger. Learning to control anger is the key.

- Express your anger in a healthy way. Don't hit, kick or push anyone or anything. If you have physical anger that must be expelled, take up a sport such as karate or kickboxing to help release your frustrations. You could also invest in a punching bag and hit it when angry.

- Express your needs. We often get angry when our needs aren't met. Always discuss your needs instead of exploding in rage. Perhaps the other person doesn't realise you are dissatisfied.
- Relax! Techniques such as deep breathing may help calm you down. When angry, take slow deep breaths until you feel calm returning.
- Practice yoga or meditation to get in touch with your inner feelings and release pent-up emotions.
- Avoid situations that increase frustration and make you uncomfortable.
- Steer clear of circumstances that reduce self-esteem. And avoid comparisons undermining your capabilities.
- Think before you act. Angry people usually react quickly to a situation, which generally leads to an overreaction. During a heated discussion, don't say the first thing that comes to mind. Think first, then speak.
- Change the way you think. This will take some practice. The next time you are getting angry, instead of swearing, say: "I'm mad but I can deal with this." Control anger – don't let it control you.

Anger is a sign of weakness. It must be controlled to gain control over our life.

◆◆◆

Control Greed

Michelangelo was one of the greatest figures of the Renaissance. Many consider his Statue of David or his painting of the Sistine Chapel ceiling in the Vatican as the finest works of art. Although highly paid, this sad, temperamental genius constantly grumbled about being short of money. He lived for nearly 90 years, but never found peace.

There is no end to a person's desires. We can be happy with little or remain dissatisfied with everything. What does a person really need? He needs a home to keep him safe and protect him from the elements, food for sustenance and clothes to cover his nakedness. But we want more than just these things. We desire to have a bigger house, no matter whether there are just three people in the family. Then we spend huge sums to embellish it. In food, we are not satisfied with simple fare. We want to sample various kinds of food, right from Continental to Chinese and Thai. As for clothes and jewellery, there is never enough.

Yet, we all know that we came empty-handed into this world and will leave empty-handed. Then why do we suffer endless tensions and problems to amass worldly acquisitions? It is simply our greed that drives us to possess more and more. We fail to realise that we become utterly stressed and miserable in pursuit of these acquisitions and acquire several diseases in the process. Control your greed, simplify your lives and life would be much happier.

Greed is the first step to unhappiness.

Don't Brood

The remedy for sorrow is to stop brooding over it. If the mind dwells on sorrow, it freshens and multiplies. One should eradicate mental suffering by wisdom and physical ailments with medicines. That is the power of intelligence, and no intelligent man should behave in a childish way. No one gifted with knowledge and understanding should ever have any inordinate clinging to youth, or physical charm or accumulated possessions, or unbroken company of friends or even health and life; for they are by their very nature impermanent. It does not befit one to sorrow long and loud for a natural misfortune.

—Mahabharata

Brooding makes things gloomier than they are. If you look at the monsoon sky, you will see grey clouds across it. A pessimist may notice the dark clouds and bemoan the fact that the sun is not in sight but an optimist may notice the silver lining in the grey clouds and revel in the cool weather. Life is what we perceive it to be. Happiness is not about having only good times but about your attitude towards life. There is no one in the world who does not face adversities. Happiness is about noticing the silver lining in the grey clouds. It is about looking at the brighter side of things.

Cultivating a blissful state is an art that can be mastered by repeated efforts. That is what the art of living is all about. A pessimist sees only the worst in everything while an optimist sees an opportunity in every reversal.

into business together. They opened a cake
ry first day they were flooded with customers.
k off rather well. The optimist said: "Well,
₂ has given us so much success right from the

ie pessimist replied: "Just think of it. If people
keep   , in like this, the door to the shop will soon become
unhingea. Ne will have to spend more in repairs than we will
profit from selling cakes."

The second friend was a true pessimist. He saw problems in opportunities! There is something known as *tempting the hubris*. When you keep saying bad things, you tempt fate to pile those bad things upon you. Conversely, when you are positive and spread good words around, the positive vibes manage to ward away trouble from your neighbourhood.

Whenever you feel low, take a walk in the park and breathe deeply of the fresh and pure air. Make an affirmation: "I am fine, everything is fine." Repeat this exercise for some time. After a while, the combination of deep breaths and affirmations is likely to lift your spirits and make you feel good.

Don't moan that the wonderful moment is over, smile that it happened. Simply get on with life. What is meant to happen will happen and what is not, won't – the important thing is not to be negative or lose heart and hope.

List five good things that happened during the day. Think about them and you will not feel gloomy any more.

◆◆◆

Be Patient

The race isn't always to the swiftest, but to those who keep on running.

—Unknown

Renowned British statesman, Benjamin Disraeli, was laughed and jeered at when he made his first speech in Parliament at the age of 32. He then said: "I will sit down now, but the time will come when you will hear me." He went on to become the Prime Minister twice! His reforms were outstanding at that time and he became very popular. In 1861, when Queen Victoria lost her husband, Prince Albert, she shut herself off from public life. It was Disraeli who persuaded her to take up public duties again.

What accounted for Disraeli's success? It was his perseverance and consistent efforts. Success eventually

rewards people who do not give up. Failures are important. It is failure that brings out the best in people. Challenges test us and bring out the inner reserves of strength that can only be tapped in times of struggle.

Henry C Beeching said: "The longest hill must end in a valley." But if we give up climbing and sit down in defeat, will we reach the valley? To rejoice and relax in attaining the goal, we must reach the valley after a stiff climb and a steep descent, no matter how tired we are. And it is patience, persistence and perseverance that will make the difference between success and failure.

Remember the age-old story of the tortoise and the hare? The diligent tortoise continued to plod relentlessly, while the fast-footed but overconfident hare fell asleep and lost the race. This story is the perfect example of how a slow, steady but patient person can succeed, while a better equipped but overconfident person fails.

Patience and perseverance pay rich dividends.

◆◆◆

Help Someone

A heart blessed with intrinsic kindness can withstand any amount of negativity. It can bounce back to a healthy, robust and positive state no matter what it goes through or no matter what goes through it. Anger, envy, frustration, hatred, anxiety, you name it, it can digest it and come clean at the end of it all.

This is all because kindness is capable of wielding great powers, even greater than the seemingly powerful emotions of anger or hatred. The power of kindness comes from its great building strength. It builds bridges of tolerance and understanding between people, between thoughts, between actions. It is at once gentle and strong. In fact, its gentleness is its greatest strength.

You can conquer the world through kindness. And that is the ultimate power of the human heart

—My Doctor

Kindness is the biggest virtue anyone can possess, as the above excerpt from the magazine, *My Doctor*, reveals. Small or big, the size of the gesture does not matter. What matters is your desire to help a person in need. It is the good intention that counts. From helping a blind man cross the road to spending some time in consoling a despondent soul, there are many little ways in which we can bring joy and happiness to others. In return our joys are multiplied.

Everyone has a busy life these days, but within those busy hours if one makes some time for a good deed, it is truly commendable.

Janet works as a tele-counsellor with an NGO. She has saved several lives by talking people out of their suicidal intentions. Once, she received a call from a desperate young boy who wanted to commit suicide because he had failed in the combined entrance test to Medical College. It was one o'clock when he began talking. Janet talked through the night till four in the morning. They spoke about everything – his relationships with parents and friends, his ambitions and dreams. By morning, the boy had changed his mind about suicide and decided to appear for the test again. Janet had yet again succeeded in saving a precious life.

A spark of hope created in a dejected heart, a ray of light provided to a destitute, tender warmth conveyed to a person in misery, a helping hand extended to a cripple – these are things which anyone can do. And the benefits are great. We find bliss in our hearts that can only come from bringing some solace to another person.

Just make up your mind to perform one good deed each day. You would have added a great drop in the ocean of humanity and, believe me, every little drop matters; nothing goes waste. As Dr Samuel Johnson said: *"He who waits to do a great deal of good at once will never do anything."*

Little drops of kindness make all the difference.

◆◆◆

Accept Criticism

Most of us dislike criticism. We only want to listen to good things about us and do not like people pointing out our mistakes or weaknesses. We bristle with indignation the moment our error is pointed out. Imagine – what if there were no book reviews by critics? We would never improve. Critics have a job to perform. They give us guidance and tell us where we failed so that we can work on those chinks and strive for perfection.

Of course, I do not suggest that you accept the malicious criticism of a jealous person. But constructive criticism is a helping hand. I take it as a big compliment when someone criticises my books – it means the critic has taken the trouble to read and then found faults. If I can improve the points brought to my notice, my books will be infinitely better.

The trick is to be positive about the entire thing. If we open our minds to criticism it does not irk us anymore. But we should not allow criticism to dent our self-confidence. Doing that would defeat our purpose.

Radha stopped painting because she could not handle the brickbats her first art exhibition produced. She began to feel she was a worthless painter. It took great persuasion and counselling from her parents and friends to restore her self-confidence. In time, she proved to be an outstanding artist as she worked hard on her weaknesses.

Use criticism to improve and grow.

◆◆◆

135

Cherish Sincere Praise

The sweetest of all sounds is praise.

—Xenophon

It is not often that people praise us. Positive feedback is our inspiration, motivation and encouragement. We require them just as we require oxygen and food. Without positive feedback we would not be able to attain our goals.

Whether child or adult, to move forward we need encouragement. When your child does well in studies, you hug and kiss him and this is the positive feedback you are giving him. The next time, this makes him strive for much better results. Similarly, when the boss compliments his worker, the latter is bound to feel pleased and work harder. We all need motivation to function better. Feedback and encouragement are doubly necessary for people who get disheartened fast and give up easily.

But a word of caution – sometimes we get taken in by flattery. There is a big difference between flattery and sincere praise. We should be able to discern between the two, if we are to believe in praise. As Wendell Phillips said: "Many men know how to flatter, few men know how to praise."

Since genuine praise is rare, it is necessary that we store this in our minds to recall later and rejuvenate our failing energies when we are tired of moving ahead.

True praise is the fuel on which our energies run.

◆◆◆

Do Your Best and Forget the Rest

We have no control over the results of what we do. We can only do our best. This is why the *Bhagavad Gita* tells us: *"Do not worry about the result; keep doing your dharma."*

Most of us perform our duties half-heartedly. When we work in the office, we expect promotions and increments. Sometimes, when we don't get the desired result, we lose heart and stop working. That is definitely not the right attitude. If we follow the teachings in the *Gita*, we would keep doing our best and someday the result of our hard work will definitely show.

Banish thoughts about the ultimate result from your mind and you will be able to perform your task with devotion and dedication. I have seen some people who do a good deed or charity, then expect some kind of recognition or adulation. By doing this, they defeat the very purpose of the charity. It is said that true charity is when the left hand does not know what the right hand is giving.

The results are never in our control because there are many factors at play that may finally determine another outcome, despite our best efforts. Don't waste time or energy worrying about the result. If we have done the job sincerely, the outcome will definitely be positive.

Whether work or charity, the real spirit lies in not thinking about the outcome but simply performing the task well.

◆◆◆

Work on Your Communication

In today's world, communication has become the most important word. In whichever field you work, good communication skills are a necessity. This is true even for human interactions. If we are unable to communicate our feelings, we are not likely to achieve the desired results. Crossed communications are the main cause of friction between people. When misunderstandings take place, they are often because the two parties failed to convey the message properly.

Here are the top three communication problems:

Manipulation: Sometimes we communicate solely for getting what we want, regardless of whether the other person can give it or not. We sulk, pout, threaten, cajole

or blackmail to make the other person feel bad. This kind of communication, though temporarily effective, has a terrible impact on the long-term health of any relationship. Respect what the other person has to offer. If they cannot give what you want, see if you can give it to yourself.

Deception: This is one of the most dangerous kinds of communication that destroys many relationships. Lies, exaggerations, games and general deceptions all cause confusion and pain. They shake the very foundation of the relationship and destroy trust. Deceptive communication should be nipped in the bud. If this sounds familiar to you, address it in your own behaviour first. When you are honest and forthright, you will no longer accept deceit from others. Honesty in communication is the most important step towards conveying thoughts effectively.

Covert Communication: Here we convey dual messages – we say one thing and do another. A prevalent form of deceit, this can take the form of promising something through actions or words and not delivering. Dual messages cause much confusion. Always pay close attention to a person's actions, which are more aligned with truth than words. If the words contradict what they are doing, ignore the words.

Any communication that comes straight from the heart and is honest will be well received.

◆◆◆

Adapt to Change

All things must change.
To something new, to something strange.

—HW Longfellow

Change is an inevitable part of life. As Lord Tennyson said: "The old order changeth, yielding place to new." Since nothing is constant on earth, change must be expected and accepted. But most people resist change. We love the times that have passed by because we are comfortable with the familiar. Each time there is change, we feel threatened and vulnerable because it is an unfamiliar zone.

In the book *Who Moved My Cheese?* Dr Spencer Johnson has dealt with the pain, adjustment and benefits of adapting to change. According to him:

- Change happens.
- Anticipate change.
- Monitor change.
- Adapt to change quickly.
- Enjoy change.
- Be ready to change quickly and enjoy it again.

The change could be about anything – attitude, people, job, residence, or locations. But each change brings about a fresh series of doubts. Often we are so settled in a groove it's difficult to get out of it. We develop roots that attach us to the place we live in, the place where we work and the people we are associated with. These roots help us remain grounded and we identify ourselves with them.

Yet, we can do nothing to stop change, which is inevitable. So we must accept and adapt to survive. Many elders keep complaining about the new generation – their attitude, the lack of respect for social norms etc. As a result, they are never comfortable in the company of youth and feel out of place. This creates severe conflicts and unhappiness. If one accepts the winds of change, life would be more comfortable. We must not stagnate but grow constantly. To grow, we must adapt ourselves to the new world order.

Adopt, adapt and adjust to change in order to survive it.

◆◆◆

Coping with Crisis

Crisis occurs in everyone's life. The difference lies in how we handle the crisis. While some of us panic, others retain their calm and handle it in a mature and wise manner.

Manju's daughter fell from their first floor balcony. Manju panicked and instead of taking the child to a doctor, she phoned her husband, who was not in his office. She then called her sister, who was out shopping. Manju wailed and kept shaking her child. The delay could have been serious. Fortunately, the neighbours came to her rescue and the child was taken to the hospital.

On the other hand, Rashi handled her husband's heart attack in a very balanced manner. Without panicking, she called up her family doctor and an ambulance and rushed her husband to the hospital. "I did feel a sense of panic rising within me when Arijeet had the attack but then I realised I had to act swiftly if I wanted to save his life, so I breathed deeply several times to get a grip over my shaking limbs and called up the doctor."

The crisis could happen at the office or at home but what matters is how we handle the situation. When we are unable to handle it adequately, it gives us a sense of despondency and misery, which adds to our problems. When we are able to handle any crisis in our work or personal life, we are more at peace and less stressed.

Keep your cool – crises are challenges thrown in your path by fate in order to test you.

Listen to Your Heart

The best and most beautiful things in the world cannot be seen or even touched. They must be felt with the heart.

—**Helen Keller**

Sometimes our hearts tell us things that our minds don't. In fact, the heart is the first thing we must listen to. You can't go wrong if you heed the heart. The world is becoming a heartless place because no one has the time or inclination to listen to the troubles of others, leave alone solve them.

When we ignore the man lying on the road, we also ignore the call of our heart. We do not want to help the person in distress because we are scared that we will be caught up for some time. But throughout the day, we feel guilty because our heart tells us that we did something wrong by rushing away when someone needed help.

Kindness is a virtue that never goes unpaid. There is a final justice delivered by God and whatever we are doing is being recorded scrupulously in His balance sheet. For each good deed we do, we are bound to receive two boons and for each bad deed, we are likely to be punished.

Our minds have become toughened with practicality and the daily grind but the heart still cares about the things we do. It will tell you when you are wrong. We could be a lot happier if we went by the heart instead of the head.

Heed your heart. It will pinpoint right from wrong.

◆◆◆

Relax and Recoup

In the fast track of life, we lose a lot of happiness. We forget to relax, recoup and tune in to our inner self. Life is not only about achieving great things but also about enjoying oneself in doing what we like. God has granted us a great life and it is up to us to make the best of it. If we live our lives only to work and earn more, we are likely to lose out on the most beautiful aspects of life. Everyone needs to relax and recoup his energies before running again. Constant running will only cause fatigue and stress.

As more people get caught up in the grind of modern living, the urgency to find antidotes is rising. Some seek spiritual gurus to overcome their stress while others resort to yoga, meditation and similar outlets. Re-energising is not only about unwinding. It is also about relaxing the mind. One requires periodic relaxation to recoup energies. It would be ideal to have one day of total relaxation after working six days. This day could be spent in outdoor activities – picnics, sightseeing or discovering nature – or in any manner that helps unwind and take the mind off immediate problems.

Alternatively, the day could be spent in lolling around the house, listening to good music, flipping through old family albums or watching television. There are some who enjoy pottering around the garden or playing games with the kids. Most people agree that religion, music, laughter and sleep are most relaxing. Whatever your way of relaxing, make it a point to allocate some time every week for leisure.

Take a regular break from the rat race. Make time for your favourite leisure activities once a week.

◆◆◆

Catch Up with Old Friends

No birth certificate is issued when a friendship is born. There is nothing tangible. There is just a feeling that your life is different and that your capacity to love and care has miraculously been enlarged without any effort on your part. It is like having a tiny apartment and somebody moves in with you, but instead of becoming cramped and crowded, the space expands and you discover rooms you never knew you had until your friend moved in with you.

—Steve Tesid

Friendship has a sublime quality that spreads sunshine through one's life. Nothing can give more joy than spending time with old friends who know us inside out. We don't have to pretend or wear masks to be with them.

In our daily lives, we don many masks and pretend to be a different person from what we are. At the office, we might be the boss, at the party we might have to act the good host even if we are not up to the task. We have to put on a smile even when we feel miserable inside.

It is only with good friends that we can let our hair down and be ourselves. We can joke, horse around and do the things we couldn't otherwise do. It is very de-stressing to be our real self. That is the reason one needs to put aside at least one evening every week to spend with friends.

Friends are forever. They help us remain cheerful and happy.

◆◆◆

Be Open to Learning

The process of learning is a constant one. At no stage of life can we stop learning or growing intellectually. If we do, we vegetate. And no one, no matter how learned, can ever say that he has learnt all and knows all.

Learning is an ocean of opportunities. We have to fathom the ocean constantly to update ourselves. Even when we are at the last stage of life, there will still be so much that we don't know. Like innumerable pearls on the seabed, there are infinite subjects in this world. We dive down and fetch one pearl, then one more and yet another but there are still many more left on the seabed.

For learning we have to open our minds and bury the ego. If not, we cannot learn or grow. Even a small child knows a lot he can teach us. For instance, he can teach us a thing or two about enjoying nature and laughing without fear. Be it a labourer or a low-paid worker, we can learn something from everyone. To think that the other person knows less than us is a fallacy.

I have learnt so much from my cook about cooking, from my gardener about plants, from the driver about cars and from my maidservant about herbal products that I could write volumes on these subjects. If I sat on my high horse and refused to gain knowledge from these people just because they were employed by me, I would be the loser. Besides, who can teach us better than these professional who have spent their entire lives working in these fields. I wonder whether any book can give us the practical knowledge that the grassroots workers can.

We do not fall in anyone's esteem when we open our minds and learn from others. In fact, we earn their respect and affection by doing so. Never stop learning in life because to survive in this world we need knowledge and this knowledge has to be constantly updated from whichever source we can find.

Learning does not stop at any stage of life.

◆◆◆

Be Your Natural Self

Most of us try to live up to others' expectations and forget to live the way we are. Our true self is hidden in a mass of others' hopes and desires. We pretend to be the people we are not. This causes us immense misery, tension and unhappiness. Putting up a pretence is a tough job. Have you noticed how your jaw aches after you have forced yourself to smile through a party? But if you were genuinely enjoying yourself and were smiling with sheer pleasure, there are no aches – just happiness.

God has created all of us in different moulds. Such is the marvel of His design that no two persons are identical in nature and looks. We are all special and must realise this. If we are simple in nature, we should be proud of

being so. If we are plain looking, we should compensate with our brains and other talents. Similarly, if we are not doing too well financially, why pretend to be rich?

Abida's husband is a pharmaceutical representative and earns enough to maintain a comfortable but modest lifestyle. Abida's friend Parveen, however, is very well-to-do since her husband is a businessman. Whenever Parveen visits Abida, the latter gets tensed trying to spruce up her home and purchasing additional foodstuff she can ill afford. This creates unpleasantness between Abida and her husband, who doesn't like wasteful expenditure.

When Abida confided to me about this problem, I asked her why didn't she behave in a natural manner. Her friend loves her because she is a nice person. Trying to match the richer friend in terms of food and lifestyle will not work. Besides, Parveen is aware that her friend has a modest lifestyle so she won't really expect much. Once Abida understood this, there was no problem and she was confident in being her normal self.

Rich or poor, fair or dark, pretty or not so pretty, we should be proud of what we have and maintain high self-esteem so that we can be our natural self. To reflect our true self is relaxing and causes no stress. Pretensions are hard to maintain and cause mental agony.

It is so much more joyful to be our natural self.

◆◆◆

Release Pent-up Emotions

Many people believe in bottling up grief and keeping emotions locked within. Crying is considered a sign of weakness, especially in men. The myth holds that men don't cry – only women and babies do.

The facts are otherwise. Crying is healthy. It is a natural process of catharsis and brings relief to a burdened and heavy heart. Crying is the ultimate expression of sadness and, on rare occasions, it is also an expression of extreme happiness. Tears can flow unpredictably when one is touched by a tender gesture. They can mist the eyes when there is relief after excessive tension.

People known to be very strong can actually be bottling up a lot of pent-up feelings. Such people are generally more stressed than those who can let the tear ducts get active once in a while.

Says 35-year-old marketing executive Abhijit: "I grew up with the belief that it was unmanly to cry. I didn't ever cry in public, but once in a while I gave vent to my emotions in private. And it brought me great relief. I envy women because they can cry freely."

It is true that women cry more easily than men. This helps them cope with emotions much more efficiently than men.

It has been observed that people sometimes feel like crying without knowing why they want to cry. It makes them feel better after they have cried for some time. Acute depression can make a person want to cry. Monday blues can make people cry. Frustrations at work or home can make people cry. The list is endless – but so are the benefits.

During Reiki training, my husband and I went through a therapy wherein students were asked to look back into the past, beginning from childhood to the present. Loud sobs were heard as people went back to their early years. Some sobbed inconsolably. Men and women – strong, sophisticated and eminent – were crying as though there was no tomorrow. At the end of the session, each person reported that s/he felt like a new person. All feelings of hurt, sadness and guilt that they had refused to let out for years, suddenly reappeared and were released.

Let me share a very poignant account narrated by a friend. This comes from a man who believed that a crying man is half a man: "Crying helped me release all the tension, anxiety and frustration of life that had built up inside me. It felt great to relieve myself of all the hurt and pain I was feeling, without being destructive. Crying is a wonderful, intimate experience I would recommend to any man. It's an experience men ought to learn to accept and share with their families. By coming to terms with my own need to cry, I now have a much better understanding of other people's feelings, but most importantly, it has strengthened and enhanced the relationship I now have with my wife and children. Put the macho stuff on hold for a while, guys. Find the strength within yourself to open up your heart and give yourself permission to cry, cry and cry.... for whatever reason. You'll come out a better man because of it."

Cry to your heart's content and let loose those lachrymals. At the end of the cathartic experience, you are sure to feel rejuvenated and refreshed.

◆◆◆

Unhappiness Causes Most Ailments

Catch hold of a peace deep within and push it into the cells of the body. With the peace will come back the health.

—Sri Aurobindo

Has anyone told you that most of our ailments are caused due to an unhappy or tense mind? When we brood incessantly, we create many health problems for ourselves. Overly tense or unhappy people are prone to heart problems, blood pressure and even arthritis. In fact, even diabetes can be stress-related. Diseases linked with our emotional state are known as psychosomatic diseases. If

we are unhappy and disturbed for a long period of time, psychosomatic diseases begin to make their presence felt.

When we are happy and joyful, the food we consume gives us pure energy and health. But when unhappy, the same food cannot help us remain healthy. Our minds are inexorably linked to our physical self.

An old adage says that a dry chapatti eaten happily is healthier than a plateful of the most expensive food eaten unhappily. Nothing could be truer. Sometimes I am amazed how wise our ancestors were. We think we are intelligent and learned but the things they have passed on to us across generations is pure wisdom.

Our body releases constant streams of various hormones and enzymes. When we are unhappy, many normal enzymes and hormones are repressed. This causes problems in the absorption of food and its nutrients. Besides, an unhappy mind plays havoc with our digestion and triggers many harmful toxins in the bloodstream. All these combine to cause health complications.

There is no point rushing to the doctor when your emotions are not under control and you are unhappy. Increase your peace of mind and all ailments will be under control.

Our health is totally dependent on our state of mind. A happy frame of mind leads to a healthy physical body.

◆◆◆

What is the Worst that Can Happen?

Has it happened to you? After worrying yourself sick over a problem you realised that it was not worth all the trouble! It has happened to me a hundred times. I have fretted over matters that really didn't become catastrophes to warrant sleepless nights.

When Saurabh's marriage was going through a bad phase, he was distraught. More than anything else, he was concerned about the fate of his little daughter. His one concern was that the ugliness of a violent marriage should not affect his child. Then he sought the advice of his spiritual guru. The guru told him to take things in his stride. "What is the worst that can happen? If your marriage breaks up, you should begin to look at life in a fresh manner. Your child will adjust to the happenings if you exhibit a positive outlook about the entire episode. Life does not stop because of a single setback. The true test of courage is during the tough times."

Saurabh soon realised that his guru was right. What is the worst that could happen? His marriage was finished anyway. Trying to hold it together and suffering mental agony was not going to help. The end was inevitable so it was better to take things in stride and deal with the matter optimistically.

We magnify most problems and work ourselves into frenzy. Things need to be seen in the right perspective. Nothing is insurmountable. God has granted a very big reserve of inner strength to all of us and we need to draw on that inner reserve in times of crisis and setbacks.

Every problem has a solution; all hurdles can be overcome. ◆◆◆

Busy People Don't Worry

If you can't fly, then run.
If you can't run, then walk.
If you can't walk, then crawl.
But whatever you do, keep moving.

—Martin Luther King, Jr

Leonardo da Vinci, renowned painter of the Mona Lisa, was the most versatile genius of all times. Once he made a mechanical lion for a play and designed the actors' costumes as well. His mind was full of ideas and his notebooks replete with drawings and plans of machines and engines of war – even a submarine and a flying machine. Leonardo was an inventive genius far ahead of his times. Do you think he had the time to worry?

Winston Churchill professed that being busy kept him from worrying. Most great personalities never had the time to worry or fret about stupid things in life. It is the idle mind that is the devil's workshop. Only when we don't have enough to keep us occupied do we worry. This is one of the reasons that most people worry at night and spend sleepless nights. Since one is lying in bed doing nothing, worries, anxieties and stress attack the mind. The mind that is preoccupied with productive thoughts does not have the time to dwell over trifles. The best way to keep from worrying is to engage in productive pursuits.

Radhika, a rich businessman's wife, was always worried about something or the other. After her children left for school and her husband for office, she had nothing to keep her mind engaged, so she worried. She worried about her husband's

155

business deals, her children's results and about everything in general. Worrying constantly took a toll on her psyche and she became depressed as days passed by. Soon, she was always high-strung and nervous.

It came to such a state that her husband took her to a psychiatrist. He had a very interesting prescription for Radhika – he suggested that she should work for a few hours daily in an orphanage he was associated with. Radhika began going to the orphanage for just three hours each morning. A few days later, she got so involved in her work and developed such strong bonds with the children that she began spending more time there.

A few months later, I couldn't recognise Radhika. She was so full of energy and bubbling with laughter. She kept talking about the little girls in the orphanage and had interesting anecdotes to relate. The transformation was incredible and there was a glow on her face. I was amazed. Radhika's association with the orphanage had given her a new meaning in life. There was no time to sit, worry or brood over things, anymore.

Keeping busy is an effective way to banish worries.

Put Your Problems in Writing

The harder the conflict, the more glorious the triumph. What we obtain too cheap, we esteem too lightly; it is dearness only that gives everything its value. I love the man who can smile in trouble, gather strength from distress and grow brave by reflection.

—Thomas Paine

It happened in 1993. I was staying along in Bangalore with my two daughters while my husband was posted in a terrorist infested area. As happens with a single parent, I was constantly worried about little things that concerned the children. While the academic result of my elder daughter was a concern, I was awash with anxiety due to my younger child's constant throat problems. She fell

sick almost every month due to tonsillitis. The ENT specialist advised a tonsil operation but I did not want this done without my husband's presence. I was seeking emotional support since I felt unable to go through the process alone.

I kept postponing the operation on some pretext or the other and my three-year-old child kept suffering. One day, unable to bear it any longer, I took her to the specialist and told him that I was ready for the operation. The operation was done; her tonsils and adenoids were removed and despite my misgivings everything went off smoothly. My child did not suffer from throat problems after that and six months later I was wondering why I had postponed the surgery for so long.

Sometimes we give too much importance to matters that don't require much deliberation. At that moment the problem seems too big but a few months later the gravity is minimised to its real state. It is like viewing something through a magnifying glass. The closer you bring the object the bigger it seems but hold it a little further and it looks much smaller. Try and study your problem in the right perspective without getting overwhelmed by its dimensions.

What seems insurmountable today may be a trifling problem tomorrow.

◆◆◆

Face the Inevitable

On many occasions we fight helplessly against a predetermined outcome. There are situations in life that are beyond our control. Trying to pre-empt things or making futile efforts in changing the course of events causes unnecessary hassles. When we know that a certain situation will end in a specified manner and our efforts will not make any difference, it is best to allow the matter to take its own course.

Lalit was working for a dot-com company in the year 2000. Those were the days when the dot-com mania was at its peak and people associated with dot-com companies were minting money. Lalit was earning triple the amount he would have earned elsewhere and he was a happy man. He had bought a swanky apartment, a new luxury car and various upmarket appliances. He had also taken several loans from finance companies for his purchases.

Then came the dot-com crash. Overnight, people were laid off without any warning. Job cuts and pink slips became the norm. Lalit lost his job along with many others. There was widespread frustration and misery amongst employees. Unable to bear their unemployment, two of them committed suicide. Several went bankrupt and suffered severe depressive ailments. Lalit lost his car and house because he couldn't pay the loan instalments he had taken. But he did not lose heart. He kept trying for another job.

It took six months of unemployment and many setbacks but he finally found a job that was enough to keep him going. In the next one year he changed two jobs till he landed a good one. "There was no point in going into depression or committing suicide. If I took the easy way out, what would have happened to my wife and child? I had to keep trying. Losing the job was an inevitable outcome of the dot-com fallout and I had to accept the inevitable. I retained a positive outlook and kept trying to find a job. I was lucky to find one and I am a happy man now."

Lalit's case is a prime example of how a person can rise above the situation. He had the wisdom to accept the inevitable and then move on. Only a person who has the tenacity to rise above disasters can be successful. We all have the capacity to triumph over adversities but we rarely try to rise up to them.

There is no point in wasting energy fighting unavoidable situations. Accept and face them with determination, then move on in life.

No one can change the inevitable. Accepting this saves undue frustration and misery.

◆◆◆

Conquer Fears and Phobias

Fear always springs from ignorance.

—Emerson

FD Roosevelt endorsed Emerson's belief and proclaimed: "The only thing we have to fear is fear itself."

In ancient times man worshipped the natural elements and animals he was afraid of, such as snakes, the sun, fire, thunder, lightning and many other things. Most of his fears stemmed from ignorance and this fact still holds true. Fear of the unknown is the worst fear. When we step into a new zone, our senses are tense and heightened and we are fearful about the outcome of every step we take.

Some people fret about things not within their control. For instance, a friend worries that he may be residing in a seismic zone and is petrified about earthquakes. He has two options: either move to a new place or just forget

about earthquakes. When it happens, it happens. What is the point of worrying oneself to death about such fears?

On the other hand, there are people who are so afraid that they resort to all kinds of magic rituals and mumbo jumbo. The mental weakness of such people pushes them to seek irrational methods to overcome their phobia.

As Sri Aurobindo put it: "It is a mistake to think that by fearing or being unhappy you can progress. Fear is always a feeling to be rejected, because what you fear is just the thing that is likely to come to you: fear attracts the object of fear. Unhappiness weakens the strength and lays one more open to the causes of unhappiness."

Aurobindo also suggests ways to control fear: "By bringing down strength and calm into the lower vital (region below the navel). Also by will and imposing calm on the system when the fear arises. It can be done in either way or both together."

In my early childhood I had a fear of speaking in public and going on stage before people. My father recognised this fear and began pushing me on public platforms either to recite or sing or dance. The first time I went on stage was quite terrible. I shook all over and fumbled my lines. But by the time I was 12 years old, I was a regular artiste and performed in many cultural events. In fact, I loved the limelight and enjoyed public adulation.

The best way to control any kind of fear is to face it squarely. As long as we avoid confronting our fears, they are likely to lurk in our lives and cause a lot of misery since we do not feel comfortable with fears. Face up to your fears with mental strength and determination. And for those who suffer excessive phobia, it is better that they consult a psychologist who will be able to analyse the cause of the phobia and help them overcome it.

Fears drag us down and stop us from performing to our peak ability.

◆◆◆

Stop Criticising

Every winner has scars.

—Herbert Casson

Reject your sense of injury and the injury itself disappears.

—Marcus Aurelius

Criticism is the pastime of unemployed and frustrated people. Those who are gainfully employed and busy pursuing their goals have no time to criticise. Most people who criticise are those unable to achieve anything in life and resentful of whatever progress others make.

"Critics are the men who have failed in literature and art," said Disraeli.

I agree with his view entirely but would alter it to read: "Critics are men who have failed." When we criticise someone unjustly, we are simply showing our jealousy. Imagine the heights people could attain if they stopped criticising others and worked on achieving their goals.

Sri Aurobindo said: "Most men are, like animals, driven by the forces of nature; whatever desires come, they fulfil them, whatever emotions come they allow them to play, whatever physical wants they have, they try to satisfy. But man also has a mind and, as he develops, he learns to control his vital and physical nature by his reason and by his will."

It is this mind that gives us power. It empowers us to grow and control our base instincts like jealousy, greed, anger etc. If we can harness our energies and direct them to positive goals, we can achieve unbelievable heights.

Consider Aruna, a homemaker. She finishes her chores by eleven o'clock in the morning and sets out for gossip sessions with likeminded women. Over several cups of tea and snacks they dissect every person in the housing complex and shred their reputation to pieces. To their shallow minds, no one is good or talented. They derive sadistic delight in running down people. For years they have done nothing but gossip about people and criticise them. The negative energies they generate could kill several people. It is not that they are uneducated or unskilled but they have not worked on their talents in a positive manner and seek an outlet for those energies in a negative way.

People like Aruna need help. They need someone to direct their energies in good work. If these women could be involved in some social cause, they could do a world of good for society.

Criticism never benefits the person who delights in criticising. Nor does it do any good to the person being criticised.

Criticism is nothing but a negative outlet for frustrated energies. It brings unhappiness and heightened frustration in its wake.

◆◆◆

Everything is Minor

Only those who will risk going too far can possibly find out how far they can go.

— TS Eliot

There is no problem in this world that deserves mental tension and agony. My husband is my biggest emotional support. He is a stable anchor and helps me maintain my equilibrium. Whenever I get tense or upset, he deflates my problem saying it is 'minor' and does not warrant any stressful thinking. This simple philosophy has helped him overcome many crises. At the height of insurgency when he was posted in Kashmir and had to deal with terrorism-related tasks, he maintained the same philosophy and overcame every problem that occurred during his three-year tenure.

Whenever we face any crises we always tell ourselves that the problem is minor and will be resolved very soon. We remind ourselves that problems are a part of life and everyone gets their share of it. Besides, God also sends help when he sends us problems. As long as you think problems are minor hiccups that will keep occurring throughout life, you will find the strength to resolve these without their taking a toll on your health. Finally, fretting and fuming or tossing sleeplessly never solves any problem. Deal with problems positively and consider them as temporary setbacks, which will disappear sooner or later. Most often, we turn little thorns of difficulties into lethal swords and subject ourselves to endless agony.

We were once stranded on the highway between the dreaded Chambal valley and Jhansi. It was midnight, a thunderstorm was raging and our car was the only vehicle on the highway. I was scared stiff and my little daughter kept crying non-stop. All the while, my husband (who must have himself been worried!) kept saying: "Don't worry. It is a minor problem and we will soon find a way out."

True to his words, a truck driver passed by and halted. The burly Sikh helped us carry out the repairs and we were on our way within an hour.

If you believe in God, remember, he will always show you the path and help you deal with problems if you don't panic. When we fret or panic, we can't deal with the situation in a positive manner. We must maintain a cool mind and the solutions will arise one after another.

Stop fretting over frivolous matters. Remain calm and the solutions will arise clearly.

Develop a Sense of Contentment

Contentment is a quality possessed by very few in this world of widespread discontent. We are never content. When we have a few thousand rupees, we want lakhs. When we have lakhs, we want millions, then billions and so on. Learning to be content with our lot is a big step towards tranquillity. Contentment is the biggest treasure ever. One may have everything one desires and yet may not find peace and contentment. While a content man needs nothing more than a plain shelter over his head, a piece of garment and simple food to satiate his hunger.

God did not create us so that we spend our entire lives chasing material comforts. Endless acquisitions only bring misery since there is no limit to acquiring. And when you get all that you wanted, will you be happy? No, sir! You will want more and the cycle will continue till your last breath.

So what should you do? You should try to cultivate contentment through the fulfilment of basic necessities. Developing contentment will leave you happy and you will enjoy each moment of your life by doing something noble rather than just acquiring material things. A content man seeks his spiritual self because his basic needs are meagre.

Gautam Buddha realised this fact, attained enlightenment and became immortal by breaking the cycle of repeated births. So have all the other enlightened people. And so can you – if you just learn to be content with your lot.

Discontentment = Misery
Contentment = Happiness

◆◆◆

Live with Your Conscience

Our conscience is the only true guide in a world full of deceit and falsity. When we follow our conscience we can never go wrong. But we constantly ignore the call of our conscience and do things contrary to its voice. But are we happy when we contravene the call of our conscience?

We can never be at peace when we ignore our conscience because it is the mirror of our soul. It shows us the right path and cautions us when we tread on the wrong one. The wise ones heed their conscience, while the foolish don't.

Some years ago, an old relative from Delhi asked me for a silk sari from Bangalore. I was busy with some project and ignored the request. I had no time to go and buy it from a shop. My conscience told me that I should buy the sari for the lady and ignore the other matters but I paid no attention to it and decided I would get it for her some other time. When I visited Delhi and she asked me about the sari, I made some excuse and placated her with an assurance that I would get it for her on my next trip.

The next trip only came about after a full year – by then the lady had passed away. I had relegated her request way down, giving my selfish reasons priority. However, I should have fulfilled the lady's request. Till date, my conscience pricks me whenever I think about her. I am suffused with a sense of guilt at my selfishness. Had I listened to my conscience this would never have happened.

This guilt comes from not heeding our conscience, which preys on our minds and brings much unhappiness in its wake. Following one's conscience is so much easier than ignoring it. While it may not always be possible to do the right thing urged by our conscience, as far as possible, sticking to the path shown by it will make us much happier.

Our conscience is the mirror of our soul. Follow its voice and you will lead a happy life.

◆◆◆

Seek Stability

The world we live in is not known for its stability. Upheavals, tragedies and calamities will occur at regular intervals and any event could alter our lives overnight. To survive in this world we need to develop personal stability and seek stabilising factors that will help us do so.

Every person lives through each day by centring himself or herself on an emotional anchor. This anchor might be a job, a relationship, a belief or even money. With this anchor, people feel secure that they will survive another day and continue to be happy. When an anchor

is present throughout life, it is seldom noticed and often taken for granted. Consequently, when an anchor is lost, our world seems to shatter as if turned upside down and inside out. Such a loss is usually unexpected and the result is extreme mental and emotional shock.

Stability does not have to come from a material object, an accomplishment, a goal, or a salary cheque. Although these things are basic to survival, emotions can be regulated in alternate ways. True stability comes from within. It rests not on personal qualities, talents, or even strengths, but on faith in oneself. It rests on the commitment one makes to stand by oneself and one's beliefs, even if everyone else has left, even if it hurts. In this commitment lies a kind of stability that can withstand any loss, any shock.

Emotional anchors that are transitory in nature will eventually vanish, leaving us high and dry. Wisdom states that the choice of our anchors should be more spiritual in nature. When we develop our spirituality and lean on that for strength and stability, we are never let down. Other kinds of anchors do not possess the sustaining power that will see us through our entire life. Friends may desert or deceive us, relationships may fade and deteriorate, money will flow in and out, and jobs will go through upheavals. But spiritual anchors will never change. They will help us cope with every adversity and remain grounded throughout the upheavals.

Spirituality is the most important stabilising factor that helps us remain grounded.

◆◆◆

Earn Goodwill and Blessings

Live for others: Those who live for others are able to achieve something beyond the reach of common people. They experience a sense of joy that comes from doing things for others. Closely related to this is service to others. It is impossible to serve others without feeling good about yourself. You don't necessarily have to do anything way out. Buy someone lunch, pass a smile, talk pleasantly to a neighbour or colleague, open doors for the aged.... the list is endless. When you have time, do some of the bigger deeds too. Volunteer at a homeless shelter, manage a food drive, donate blood or do some such deed that you can handle. Serving others is a great way to happiness.

Care and share: Have you ever experienced the joys of giving? People who live only for themselves are amongst the unhappiest ones, while those who have little but share these modest possessions are the happiest. Sharing brings a sense of fulfilment and joy that nothing else can bring.

When we are considerate and caring, we do ourselves much good. You will be surprised at how much good we do ourselves when we do something for others. Whatever good we do for someone usually returns manifold. That is the law of Nature. If you give a rupee, it is bound to come back many times over. If you don't believe this, try it out. Besides the monetary return, the good deed benefits us in many more ways. It ensures peace and joy – the biggest return one can get. There is no wiser investment than love because it is returned with heavy interest.

Life is a joy for those who believe in caring and sharing.

◆◆◆

Read Something Inspiring Each Day

Why did our ancestors begin their day with prayers and shlokas? No prizes for guessing. It's well known that every hymn and shloka we recite spreads positive vibes in our environment and brings peace and happiness. Similarly, when we are feeling low, inspirational stories impart peace to our minds besides giving fresh impetus to face adversities.

When I lost my mother and went through a very bad emotional phase, a friend presented me with *Kane and Abel*. It is a book about two strong men who fight all adversities to turn their life into a big success. It dealt with emotional matters that overtook the two at various

stages of their lives. I found the book highly inspirational because it illustrated how a person could strengthen himself and go on with life. I recovered from my gloom and went on to deal with life in a more positive manner.

Many people read the *Bhagavad Gita* and try to follow its sayings. It gives them much hope and strength. Similarly, people read the *Bible* and try to practice its precepts. These are books that have stood the test of time and shown the right path to millions, especially when they are facing crises in their lives.

Years ago, when I commuted to work by a chartered bus in Delhi, I found people reading some such book to begin their day in peace. I also adopted the habit and found myself ready to face any kind of problem throughout the day. The inspirational reading gave me the strength and courage to face all adversities and keep my cool. It taught me to take one day at a time and deal with problems optimistically.

In our daily lives, when we read inspirational thoughts we are motivated to do our best and achieve positive results during the day. You too can begin doing so – today!

When the road ahead seems dark and there is no light at the end of the tunnel, read inspirational books. Acting like beacons, they will lead you to illumination.

Forego Revenge

In taking revenge a man is but equal to his enemy, but in passing it over he is his superior.

—Bacon

When we harbour resentment and seek revenge, we are doing the greatest disservice to ourselves. Revenge is for the petty-minded. It does not bring any satisfaction but stokes more hatred and fuels further unhappiness in the person who seeks it.

Mahatma Gandhi said: "If someone slaps you on one cheek, offer him the other." The Mahatma was echoing what Jesus Christ had first said over 2,000 years ago. Turning the other cheek is meant to shame the person. If we slap the aggressor in retaliation, he will slap us once again and the battle will linger on. Have you not seen street fights where two sides keep arguing and fighting until they resort to fisticuffs that sometimes lead to bloodshed?

Hate and revenge are totally negative, ensuring unhappiness and breeding bitterness. A strong man has the ability to forgive and this act ennobles his soul. The fire of revenge rages in the bosom of the unwise. It never brings any satisfaction or happiness.

Vendetta and revenge breed misery and unhappiness.

◆◆◆

Live with Nature

Nature never did betray
The heart that loved her.

—William Wordsworth

The best and most beautiful things in the world cannot be seen or even touched. They must be felt with the heart.

—Helen Keller

In a study conducted over 17 years by Dr Mario Vaz, Director of Nutrition, St. John's National Academy of Health Sciences, Bangalore, he found that aged persons in rural areas were psychologically and physically stronger than those living in urban areas. He found that the urban elderly were eight times more vulnerable to diabetes, five times more susceptible to blood pressure and two times more prone to heart diseases than their rural counterparts. The rural elderly were also three and a half times less susceptible to depression.

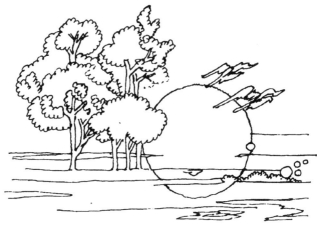

Dr Vaz opines that the gradual shrinking of green cover in cities has led to a decrease in the resistance levels of individuals. Living amidst nature provides our minds and bodies with bountiful benefits that offset pollution and stress factors. Nature's bounties cannot be compensated by the comforts of modern living. When we commune with nature, spend time watching the birds and enjoy the fragrance of flowers, our minds relax completely and we feel sheer joy pervade us. The pure and fresh air, gurgling waters of the stream and the clear blue skies are rejuvenating elements that can work their magic on any tired mind.

Man is a part of nature and isolating ourselves from it brings tension and unhappiness. We are much happier when surrounded by flora and fauna. This is why most people take off for a hill station or the seacoast for a holiday to unwind, relax and rejuvenate.

Since it is not possible to stay in such places forever, what does one do? We could try to recreate a part of the natural beauty in our homes. The little green cover in front of the house or in the backyard can be converted into a small garden or a vegetable patch. The joy that comes each time you plant a sapling and see it bear flowers or fruit is something beyond words.

In fact, gardening is a good de-stressor. Planting a tree is a great source of happiness. Imagine a sapling that you planted a few years ago now becoming a big, healthy and robust tree where birds build nests and sing in joy, ushering each new dawn with a welcome tune. Bees and other insects nestle in its branches. Won't it provide you a sense of great achievement and joy? It is almost akin to raising a child and watching it grow strong and handsome.

Nature is one of the greatest sources of joy.

◆◆◆

Zip Your Lip

Keep thy tongue from evil and thy lips from speaking guile.
—Psalms, XXXIV.13

Don't say the wrong things or hurt anyone. Words and deeds have a way of getting back at you. Words are like arrows or bullets, once shot they cannot be retrieved. If you hurt someone with harsh words, those words will get back at you sooner or later.

It is better to zip the lip and say nothing than to utter wrong words. No one who hurts others lives in peace. In some manner or the other, at some time or the other, he is bound to suffer. This is an inviolate truth of life.

Just recall the times you caused someone misery through harsh words. It brought you some satisfaction then, but later, the hurt and grief of the person haunted you.

Roshini was extremely petty and sharp-tongued. She spared no one and was unkind to all friends. Most people avoided her. As a young girl she got away with her nasty words. When she got married, she found a match in her mother-in-law who was more foul-mouthed! The two delighted in hurting each other and traded sharp words. Eventually Roshini could take it no longer and changed her ways. She tried to hold her tongue and soon realised she had a much better relationship with all her friends than ever before. Today, she is a reformed person.

Think before you speak. Sharp words can hurt you more than anyone else.

◆◆◆

Count Your Blessings

As a child, a Hindi film song sung by Mukesh fascinated me: *Bahut diya dene wale ne tujhko, anchal hi na samaye to kya kije.* (The Almighty has given you a lot, if it does not fit into your receptacle, what is to be done?) This song remains embedded in my mind till today. Whenever I feel depressed because something has gone wrong, I hum this song and feel stronger immediately. The lyrics convey what most learned people have said. God has given us a lot. It is our greed for more that does not make us realise His generosity. We never thank Him for the healthy limbs and the keen mind that He has given us but curse our fate for the adversities that come our way. If we were to make an honest list of the blessings endowed on us, the list would run long.

We tend to forget the good things that we have been granted by God. A loving family, comfortable living conditions, a secure job and a safe haven we call home are so easily taken for granted till we stop to think about people who are not fortunate enough to possess these. We constantly desire materialistic things without even fully utilising the ones we have.

The moment we stop taking nature's gifts for granted and begin appreciating the wealth of these important gifts, we can truly achieve a lot of happiness and peace.

Spending a few moments in thanksgiving each day makes us realise our good fortune.

◆◆◆

Beat Depression
and Become Cheerful

Let's face it, it happens to the best of us. There are days when you simply can't function normally and the funniest thing is that, most often, you can't even come up with the reason for that down-and-out feeling. Feeling blue once in a while is perfectly normal. Life is all about that strange yo-yo phenomenon which is so perplexing and confusing: up one moment and down the other. Cheer up! There are ways and means to beat that feeling of gloom and doom.

Tap it up: How about dancing away your blues? Dancing is supposed to be a fantastic exercise that releases those feel-good hormones and gets your juices flowing. Fast-paced music blows away depressive feelings. In case you don't want to dance, you can sing or play some musical instrument.

Flower power: Bring those crystal vases out. Flowers are good. They can bring back the sunshine into your life. Can there be a more effective element than some sunflowers to bring sunshine back into your life? They combine the healing effects of both colour therapy and aromatherapy – and who can remain gloomy after the double dose of cheer?

Colour code: Colour therapy is very effective. You could wear the colours or use them in the interiors of your home or just place some interesting objects in the recommended colours. For those lacking zing and zest, colour therapy advocates the use of **red**, which is the colour of energy, vitality and power. It will help get rid of depression. **Green** – the colour of harmony and balance – is good for tired nerves and helps elevate the mood. It will balance the emotions and bring about a feeling of calmness.

You could also try **blue**, which is the colour of truth, serenity and harmony. Blue is good for cooling, calming, and soothing the mind. Then there is **lavender**, the colour of equilibrium that helps with spiritual healing and can be used as a tranquilliser to aid sleep.

Clean up clutter: Carrying emotional garbage is like carrying an unmanageable load of rubbish on the head. You don't want to carry extra baggage that will damage your psyche and make you feel blue throughout life. Emotional clutter can be even more damaging, so discover ways to correct those mistakes. Do anything if you can correct them and if that is not possible, forgive yourself and toss it out of your life.

Take a break: Maybe you just have been working too hard or maybe you are stuck in a rut. A break gives a person the much-needed breather and ensures a fresh perspective on problems. Take stock of the situation. If you feel the present job is frustrating, it's time to look for another.

Fun-n-frolic: How long since you did something outrageous? If you have been leading a staid life, dark moods will continue to cloud your life. Experiment with outlandish ideas and learn to laugh at yourself. Research shows that children laugh approximately 400 times a day but adults laugh only about 20 times a day. Laugh like a child!

Positive power: There's dynamic power in positive thinking. If you think good things are just around the corner, you will feel brighter and more cheerful. And you will also find good things around the corner! When you leave the house each morning, just tell yourself a couple of times: "I'm going to have a great day and nothing can stop me from doing so." It is amazing what you can achieve.

Thank God: Express your gratitude to the Almighty for all that He has given you. Write down half-a-dozen things everyday that you are grateful for – right from perfectly functioning limbs to a loving family, the flowers, birds and nature. This cannot fail to cheer you up.

Friendly support: Take a day out with old friends. Spending time with friends who know you intimately will help you be yourself. You will come away feeling younger, more positive and more excited about life than you were before you met up. Invite them over to share a bite and catch up on each others' lives. This is the best rejuvenator.

Kid stuff: Spend time with children, who have an incredible capacity for spreading cheer and joy. No one can remain unaffected in their joyous company. They could teach you a thing or two about the joy of living.

Be a student: Take music lessons, learn to make your own dresses or do your decorating. Catch up with the latest in computers or simply start painting. Initially, if you are not confident, do this for your own eyes. Visualise the end product of your efforts and imagine the changes it could bring in your life. Follow it till the end. An added bonus will be your increased self-esteem.

Seek solutions: A nagging problem can be most depressing. It could be a frustrating job, a bad relationship, or some health problem. Get cracking and find solutions to the problems, no matter how minor or major. Talk over your problems with a confidante. If that is not possible, do an Internet search through any of the search engines by typing related terms and find out a Net support group.

Life is all about living with joy and enjoyment. Each moment is a special one because the present moment will never return in your life. So make the best of it and stop feeling dejected just because something went wrong somewhere.

Remember, nothing is more important than happiness.

◆◆◆

20 Tips for Happiness

1. There is calmness within all of us.
2. The mind is peaceful until made to be otherwise.
3. Believe you have the right to be happy.
4. Realise that every feeling you have is preceded by a thought.
5. Be aware of the bewildering array of ego pursuits that surround us.
6. Surround yourself with positive people.
7. Know that you were created to be content.
8. Know that nothing has to go right for you to be at peace.
9. Remember that there are no permanent mistakes.

10. Accept others as they are. Help when a way to help is clear. See innocence in mistakes.
11. Remember that haste creates unhappiness. Give yourself more time to do things.
12. Identify people and places that cause unhappiness.
13. Avoid working to defeat people who disagree with you.
14. Forgive. Know that to forgive you need do nothing; it is an act of the heart, not the body.
15. Know that when any judgmental train of thought ends, the damage it caused to the mind ends with it.
16. Try to look upon the world the way we allow ourselves to look at a child.
17. Work to enjoy the present.
18. Realise that everyone has the key to being content but few use it. The key is our undeveloped mental focus.
19. Avoid the motto *Do little and expect much.* Trade it in for *Work hard but expect little.*
20. Remember, a gentle vision makes a gentler world.

Inspirational Quotes

Remember your possibilities; forget your limitations,
Remember your potentialities; forget your
restrictions,
Remember you abilities; forget your disabilities,
Remember your assets; forget your liabilities,
Remember your strength; forget your weakness,
Remember your joys; forget your sorrows.

—William Arthur Ward

But there was no need to be ashamed of tears, for
tears bore witness that a man had the greatest of
courage, the courage to suffer.

—From *Man's Search For Meaning* **by Victor Frankl**

When things go wrong, as they sometimes will,
When the road you're treading seems all up-hill.
When the funds are low, and the debts are high,
When you want to smile but you have to sigh.
When care is pressing you down a bit,
Rest if you must but don't you quit.
Success is failure, turned inside out,
The silver tint of the clouds of doubt.
And you never can tell
How close you are,
It may be near when it seems afar.
So stick to the fight when you're hardest hit;
It's when things go wrong that you
MUST NOT QUIT.
It's never too late to be what you might have been.

—George Eliot

The secret of success is learning how to use pain and pleasure instead of having pain and pleasure use you. If you do that, you're in control of your life.

—Anthony Robbins

Difficult times have helped me to understand better than before how infinitely rich and beautiful life is in every way and that so many things that one goes worrying about are of no importance whatsoever.

Isak Dinesen

By being happy we sow anonymous benefits upon the world.

—Robert Louis Stevenson

What is to give light must endure burning.

—Victor Frankl

◆◆◆

Epilogue

Many people in the world would give anything for a little happiness and tranquillity. Happiness and peace of mind seem to have deserted most people. Success, wealth, fame and adulation definitely come at a very steep price. The rush for living life to the hilt can be disastrous. Just as there are umpteen ways to get rich quickly and pundits who will sell you "secrets" to attain this for a price, there are an equal numbers of gurus who will direct you on the path to *nirvana*. Again for a steep price! Nothing comes without a price tag, not even peace.

The truth is there are no shortcuts or easy methods; in fact, it is easier to amass wealth today than to attain peace of mind. This is not available in the market nor can it be bought off the shelf. You have to work towards it. This book will help readers do just that by pointing out the right path. But having read the book, you will now have to practise these guidelines.

As I said, there are no shortcuts in life....

SECRETS OF
MIND POWER

—Harry Lorayne

Do you want to be successful?
Are you ready to improve yourself?
Looking for a better and happier life?

Of course the answer is YES! You have the desire and now, here are the ways by which you can achieve these goals. With Harry Lorayne's proven methods — from the world's foremost authority on memory training — you will learn how to organize and develop the hidden powers of your mind!

This is the first revised edition of the famous best-seller, *Secrets of Mind Power*. It is Lorayne's 14th book on the subject of memory. You are treated to the proven techniques and methods of a professional, as you are shown how to use your mind to its fullest capacity.

Here is a sampling of the benefits you will receive:

- ❖ Increasing your powers of memory and concentration
- ❖ Strengthening good habits and discarding bad ones
- ❖ Becoming an effective public speaker
- ❖ Conquering fear
- ❖ Taking on a new attitude and approach to life
- ❖ Improving your powers of observation
- ❖ Making friends easily and quickly
- ❖ Thinking logically, effectively and creatively
- ❖ Learning to trust others
- ❖ Becoming more organized and time-efficient

Demy Size • Pages: 184
Price: Rs. 96/- • Postage: Rs. 15/-

How to remain Ever Happy

—M.K. Gupta

Fight back the Negativity and be Positive

Today's life is full of tensions. Consumerism, competition and mad scramble for more and more, are weighing down heavily on everybody — creating stress, anxiety and depression. We're as if caught in a web of own making. Is there a way out? YES!

How to Remain Ever Happy is an honest attempt to analyse these problems and offer over 101 effective solutions. Covering different facets of the problem, it suggests *positive approach and planned thinking* to achieve the impossible.

The sound advice includes:
- ❖ Eat healthy, live better
- ❖ Be above narrow considerations
- ❖ Cultivate optimism
- ❖ Learn to say 'No'
- ❖ Don't get into the rat-race
- ❖ Keep on working even if upset

And a whole lot of sure-shot tips to relieve yourself from tension. Well-illustrated and thoroughly researched, the book is a sure key to happiness.

Demy size • Pages: 156
Price: Rs. 68/- • Postage: Rs. 10/-

From Despair to Joy

—*A.P. Sharma*

Familiar Ways to
Attain HAPPINESS

If happiness were a myth, the Buddha would never be able to accomplish it. Neither Ramkrishna, Vivekananda, Gandhi or other, who followed the road to the impersonal love, would ever get it. The path leading to impersonal love is surely difficult, but nothing could be achieved without following the right path and the right means.

Happiness can be achieved if one can cultivate 'silence' of the mind. That silence can be attained by proper awareness. It can be reached by keeping the mind totally alert so that it acts like an observer who works without interfering with the others. Happiness·can surely be obtained by keeping the mind's energy intact, without wasting it in insignificant matters. It can be obtained by meditation and prayers or by any informal procedure too, provided one is able to keep one's mind alert and free from mental fetters.

Demy size, Pages: 104
Price: Rs. 80/- • Postage: Rs. 15/-

The Joy of Natural Living

—Luis S.R. Vas & Anita S.R. Vas

The Joy of Natural Living incorporates research findings on health, psychology, body care and spirituality which emphasise the benefits of natural living. A common theme runs through all the material gathered here. —the more you rely on nature and nature therapy in dealing with your physical and mental problems, the more joy you get out of life.

The authors hope the reader will be able to regain natural joy by experimenting with some of the advice from experts prese.:ted here which include:

✦ Coping with stress through relaxation techniques and Pleasant and Positive thoughts.

✦ Role of diet in achieving mental & physical well being.

✦ Safe & successful physical activity program.

✦ Natural grooming and herbal preparation to attain increased self-confidence

---

Demy size, Pages: 152
Price: Rs. 80/- • Postage: Rs. 15/-

The Secrets of Marital Bliss

—*Tanushree Podder & Ajoy Podder*

**The secrets of marital harmony &
tips to tide over marital discord**

Research shows that happily married persons live longer than single ones. And couples in a happy marriage have a healthy constitution, mentally, emotionally and physically. Despite such facts, separations and divorces are rising every year.

If happy marriages ensure fulfillment and a sense of security, shouldn't couples be working towards strengthening their marriage? Research indicates that the most successful Indians around the globe have succeeded because of strong family values and support systems.

The Secrets of Merital Bliss gives readers practical guidelines on how to overcome daily hurdles and live in peace and harmony. The book deals with the pitfalls that appear at various stages of married life. Married and unmarried couples of all ages must read this book to ensure peace, stability and harmony in their relationship.

Demy size • Pages: 176
Price: Rs. 80/- • Postage: Rs. 15/-